Praise for *Silent Maine Reminc*

Lt. Col. Dave Grossman, United States Army, Retired
Author of *On Killing* and *On Combat* remarks to Alden Weigelt concerning his new work *Silent Maine Reminders:*

> "Wow. What a superb piece of writing, my brother wordsmith! I enjoyed this very much. A powerful, eloquent, and deeply moving book. This book preserves and enshrines, in humble words, the extraordinary contributions of humble, ordinary citizens in our nation's time of need, across the centuries. As J.R.R. Tolkien put it in *The Lord of the Rings*:
>
> > Not all that is gold doth glitter,
> > Not all those who wander are lost.
> > The old that is strong does not wither,
> > And the deep roots are not touched by the frost.
>
> This book permits us to tap the strength that is drawn from those deep roots that have endured the bitter frost in centuries past. In these pages we can seek out the old that is strong and does not wither, in order to meet the challenges of our current age.
> Well done!"

Central Maine movie critic, columnist, and former Hollywood actor Gerald (J.P.) Devine remarks:

> "Writer and police officer Alden L. Weigelt's new book *Silent Maine Reminders* is anything but silent. Weigelt takes us from his own story growing up in Waterville, where his family ran the popular Preble Studio, to a real-life Maine war hero, Estol 'Mack' McClintock, whose life echoed the fictional story told in *Saving Private Ryan*. McClintock was a veteran and survivor of the famous 'Big Red One' 1st Infantry Division. A moving tale."
>
> "Weigelt's book is really a tapestry of Maine faces and voices. He paints all his scenes in vivid color."
>
> "But many of the stories simply reflect the history of the everyday lives of ordinary Mainers, who through public service and spiritual commitment, forged a thread from the American Civil War to the writer's own adventures on the modern streets of London, England."
>
> "Weigelt's citizens are portrayed honestly and vividly and give us an insight into the 'Common Man.'"

SILENT MAINE REMINDERS

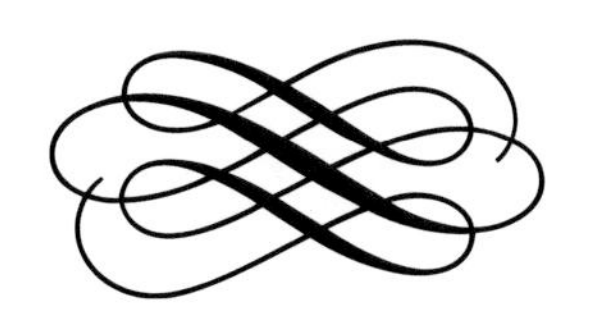

ALDEN L. WEIGELT

Silent Maine Reminders

ISBN: 978-1-936447-14-5

Cover Designed by Kris McKenna

Book Designed and Produced by
Maine Authors Publishing
558 Main Street, Rockland, Maine 04841
www.maineauthorspublishing.com

This work is dedicated to those special few, past and present,
who, for the sacred principles of righteousness, justice,
and freedom, have chosen to stand in the way of danger for the
many who could not or would not stand there for themselves.

To: CHERYL

WITH MY BEST WISHES,

LOVE,

ALDEN L. WEIGELT

9/22/2012

Contents

Acknowledgments

This project would not have been possible without the great contribution of information provided by the following individuals. All of these people contributed by confirming the accuracy of the topic discussed, and most were actual participants in the history documented. It was a joy to interview them all, and they are all partners in confirming and preserving these sacred memories of service and sacrifice.

Capt. Gerald J. Adler
Richard Olin
Tia LaMarre Dupler, RN
George C. Brown
Dr. Timothy Setzer, DD
Steve Libby
Arnold Carter
Bruce Siviski
Dr. Joseph A. Marshall, MD
Markham L. Gartley
Maj. Tommy Towery
Yeoman Warder Kenneth McGrath
Lt. Col. Don Harris
Dr. Earl E. Weigelt, DD
CAPT John E. Morris
Marion B. Jackins
Rev. Kevin LaMarre
RMC Kenneth Bernard
Peter Pratt
Dr. Ann LeBlanc, PhD
Lt. Col. Dante E. Bulli
Earle G. Shettleworth, Jr.
MSgt. William A. Lindie, Jr.
Real Cyr
Dr. Alan Slack, DVM
CSM Estol R. McClintock
David Gibbs
SFC Brian D. Wedge
Norman McKinstry
Patricia Hross
Harold (Dusty) Woodside

(Note: Rank or distinction of title included before or after the person's name illustrates that the person fully retired with or is currently serving with this rank or distinction.)

I appreciate all the help that my friend Keith Ploufe provided with the initial edit of this project. I especially appreciate Keith's patience in making his point in areas where we definitely disagreed. Keith is a retired veteran of the United States Air Force, who went on to continue serving that *something, greater than himself,* as did the ones spoken of in Chapter 12, *Is There Something in Their Genetics?*

I thank my friend and fellow police officer Kris McKenna for his work with the cover of this book. I also thank Kris and our fellow officers of the Waterville Police Department and my brothers on the other side of the pond, Ken McGrath of Her Majesty's Palace and Fortress, the Tower of London, as well as counterterror specialists Brian and Russ for their encouragement, enthusiasm, and support for this project. They are all examples of warriors who "get it"!

I acknowledge my Aunt Marion, my brother Robert, and the rest of my family. I especially acknowledge my parents, who have now passed. Mom and Dad, your values survive and are alive today in two more successive generations.

Most of all, I thank my Lord and Savior for my wife Debora. She is the love of my life and a woman I truly don't deserve.

"We don't have to turn to our history books for heroes. They are all around us."

—Ronald Reagan, State of the Union Address, January 26, 1982

"Greater love hath no man than this, that a man lay down his life for his friends."

—Jesus Christ, John 15:13 KJV

Introduction

Have you ever walked or driven by a cemetery in Maine or somewhere else in our great nation in late May and glimpsed those small flags above those resting there? And if you walked through the cemetery, did you note the small, metal flag holders with various emblems and wonder what those emblems meant? Do you know what the letters "GAR" stand for on many of these flag holders, and their significance, especially in Maine?

Have you ever gone to an air show and seen military planes from the past and glimpsed a tear or two on the cheeks of some of the older members of the audience and wondered what memory was stirred? Have you ever been to a parade and witnessed as the "Colors" passed how some responded the same way? Perhaps you even experienced a lump in your own throat as they passed, or, at the least, in response to the effect the Colors had on others.

Have you ever dared to thank the old gentleman with the baseball cap proclaiming that he is a WWII veteran for his service? Have you ever thanked the one with the cap declaring he is a Vietnam veteran for *his* service?

Have you ever looked closer at the statue in the park or a plaque in the town or city square and read what is written there? Have you ever considered why there are so many cannons, statues, and monuments, many the same, in our Maine cities and towns? Have you ever even taken the time to consider? These are examples of silent reminders of people and events. When these events happened, our memories were fresh, but oh how quickly our memories fade. They fade until that reminder is no longer heard or understood anymore. To those who simply pass by, the reminder that at one time may have spoken volumes is silent. If you pause and take the time, the reminder that was at first silent may begin to speak. We only need to listen. Maybe you will want to learn more.

This is a story about people and their connections to each other and events, both local and global. Some of the people are still living and some are now dead. We know the names of several, but there are many more names—too many—that we do not know. They are ordinary everyday people just like us. They lived; they loved; and many raised families, though others never got the chance. Living at different times in history, they all had one thing in common: they all believed in something greater than themselves. They put others first and many stood in the way of oncoming danger for those who could not or would not stand there for themselves. In a present generation that seems obsessed with self, there are still those who believe in that greater something and would risk everything to preserve it.

It is often said that fact is stranger than fiction. I believe that reality is always more interesting and more spectacular than fiction. I grew up steeped in the reality of the events and people in this book as a citizen of the United States, in Maine and the Waterville area. These stories surrounded and shaped me profoundly.

These people, past and present, are the guardians of our freedom. It is these that we need to remember, and their reminders are all around us. The reminders are many. It may be a monument, a building, a grave, a piece of equipment, or just a place. We only need to learn and remember what they represent and then choose to appreciate it. The reminders are only silent if we choose to ignore them.

Sentimental Journey. (Photo by Alden Weigelt)

Chapter 1

SENTIMENTAL JOURNEY

My journey exploring Maine's silent reminders began on July 15, 2006. My wife, Debora, and I had the honor of babysitting our first grandchild, nine-month-old Lana, for the day. We decided to take her for a ride and visit the Hancock County–Bar Harbor Airport in Trenton, Maine. A friend of mine had told me there was a B-17 Flying Fortress on display at the airport for a few weeks. The B-17 was a heavy strategic bomber of World War II. The crews that manned them, on average, were only 22 years old.

There were two reasons for this field trip. The first was because I have always been interested in airplanes. I took flying lessons my junior and senior years of high school in the '70s, and earned a private pilot certificate the summer of my graduation. I married my high school sweetheart, Debora, two years later, right after we both earned our associate degrees in our chosen fields. The responsibilities of marriage and family soon put a limit on my flying allowance, and, since flying was more of a hobby and not a means to a living, I had to indulge in it sparingly. I never owned my own plane, but Debora was kind enough to let me keep my hand in over the years by renting airplanes.

There were gaps in the periods that I indulged my hobby, such as when the bills demanded it. However, over the years, I was able to log a little over two hundred hours of flight time. When the kids got old enough to go with me, I found a new justification for my hobby—to expose them to flight and, hopefully, awaken a passion for aviation in them while continuing to satisfy my own. I hoped to also pass my fascination for flight on to my grandchildren.

The second reason for the field trip was my lifelong interest in history. I was born just eleven years after World War II. My parents were of the generation that Tom Brokaw referred to as *The Greatest Generation* in his 1998 best seller. My parents met and married during the Great Depression and started their family during the war. They raised me to appreciate and respect the values of those who struggled to survive during that most desperate of times.

My dad worked in one of the brokerage houses on Wall Street when the stock market crashed on Black Thursday, October 24, 1929. He told me about people he knew who had jumped out of windows to their deaths a few days after the crash. With the financial world in ruins, my dad moved to Maine the next spring, where he later met my mother. He went on to help build Liberty Ships in South Portland, Maine. My mother, Myrtle (Jackins) Weigelt, worked in the Civil Defense Warning Center in Waterville, Maine, in addition to her regular job working for the Preble Studio in Waterville.

My aunt, Marion Jackins, joined the Civilian Motor Corps and learned to drive an ambulance. After the war, she never drove again. She also never married. It is of note that many men never came home from World War II. Would life have been different for Aunt Marion had there not been a war? What opportunities were lost for her because of the sacrifices of so many others?

My maternal grandparents, Alden and Bessie Jackins, lived on Winter Street in Waterville, where I grew up. They raised a son and two daughters there. Their home was one of those neighborhood hubs that people seemed drawn to. Many of my grandparents' friends, as well as their children's friends, often visited and ate with them long before I was born. Family and friends ate at the same table as the boarders my grandmother took in, a table that I would later eat at growing up. Some of these people saw war, and one neighbor never came home again.

My grandparents had three children: a son, Prescott, and his sisters, Myrtle (my mother) and Marion. Some of the men who came or stayed at the Jackins house were friends of the children and others were boyfriends of the daughters. They all loved my grandparents. Years before I was born, one World War I veteran from Lincoln, Maine, visited often to spend time with my grandparents as he continued his lifelong recovery from his experiences as an army ambulance attendant in the "Great War." That was the war referred to as the "war to end all wars." Well, it didn't. Two decades later, the world experienced one of the most horrific wars in human history. The WW I vet my grandparents provided periodic sanctuary to later became a successful undertaker in Lincoln, but he continued to return and visit his friends who had been there for him so long ago.

I was born after my maternal grandfather passed away. I never knew him. I grew up knowing some of the men who still came by to visit my grandmother, but at that time I knew none of their stories of war. Most of these men referred to my grandmother as "Ma Jackins." I remember two of the close friends of the family who had honorably served in combat during World War II, and they were both alcoholics. They continued to visit the house on Winter Street for the rest of their lives. They were accepted there and they loved my grandmother. And our story was not unique. Most of my friends had family or friends that served, preserving freedom, in World War II, a war that cost the world more than 72 million lives.

The 15th was a beautiful July day in 2006. It was warm with a high, thin overcast. We arrived in Trenton in the late morning and found the B-17 on display. The name painted on the aircraft nose was *Sentimental Journey* along with a pin-up likeness of Betty Grable giving one last backward glance to the brave airman who would fly its perilous missions. The Commemorative Air Force owns *Sentimental Journey,* and the vintage aircraft tours the country every summer. The Commemorative Air Force is a nonprofit organization interested in preserving historical aircraft, mainly from World War II. They have chapters all over the United States and have several examples of old war birds in their collection. I had seen B-17s before at air shows, but never had the opportunity to tour one.

The members of the Commemorative Air Force had set up a line at the front of the aircraft where you could pay five dollars, take a self-guided tour through the front of the aircraft, and then exit at the rear. The B-17 has a small hatch under the nose that the forward members of the aircrew used for boarding. If you ever saw the movie *Twelve O'Clock High* or *Memphis Belle*, you can imagine the crewmember throwing his parachute and other equipment over his head and up through the hatch, grabbing the edge of the hatch opening with both hands to swing his legs up through, and hauling up the rest of his body. We were not to enter in this way, but rather our entry was by means of an aluminum stepladder that had been erected for the use of the tourists.

Though I wasn't thinking of it at the time, it had been almost ten years to the day since I had last logged any hours as pilot in command. My flying hobby had taken another lapse as we began putting the first of our three children through college. It was the child of our firstborn, our son, who we had with us today, and she remained in her carriage at the front of the aircraft with her grandmother as I boarded.

They say that the sense of smell is a powerful evoker of memories. It can be more powerful than any other sense, including sight, because it goes straight to certain memory centers with little processing. I must say that, in my case, this is true. As I climbed the ladder and entered through the hatch, I was suddenly struck with the familiar smells of high octane AvGas mixed with oil, fabric insulation, and wiring. Any pilot is familiar with the smell of an airplane that has been sitting on the ramp and baking in the sun. And yes, they somehow all smell the same and may stir similar sentiments in the beholder.

The second thought that struck me was that, when these aircraft were in service, I wondered, how many young men had entered the craft in the traditional way without the aid of a stepladder? I also wondered how many young men had jumped through a similar hatch in terror to desperately escape a dying ship. The B-17 was a weapon of war, and many had sacrificed themselves to wage it for the freedom that I enjoy.

As I climbed into the airplane, I felt a tremble, as I was now in hallowed and consecrated space and somehow unworthy to be where so many had worked and died while they helped save the world. Remember, not only did the young heroes that flew in them do so facing a determined enemy that was trying to kill them, but they did so in almost unbearable conditions. This airplane is not pressurized, and the kids that flew in them did so while breathing oxygen through a mask. They kept warm wearing bulky electric blanket–style suits because outside, at 20,000 feet, it's 12 degrees below zero. And at 25,000, it's minus 30.

I continued my tour through the aircraft. I saw the bombardier and navigator station in the nose and traveled through the flight deck. I moved aft to the bomb bay and then back to the radio compartment. After walking through the waist-gun area behind the wings, I exited the airplane through a small door in the rear. I overheard one of the Commemorative Air Force colonels answering questions for another tourist. I caught a statement made by the colonel that his father had served in a plane just like this.

For those who took time to read it, there was a small sign that provided a brief history of the airplane. Boeing made about 12,000 B-17s. Of those produced, about one-third, or 4,000, were shot down. I knew that each airplane had a crew of ten, and the math revealed that in this single weapon platform, 40,000 American servicemen had been shot down while defending my freedom though I was not yet born. I walked back and spoke with the colonel for a few minutes to make sure that I understood correctly what I had just read. I also learned that *Sentimental*

Journey would be flying the following day, taking up to eight guests for a forty-five-minute ride. The cost of the ride equaled about a week's pay for me.

I found Deb and Lana and took some pictures of them with the airplane from different angles. I finally dared to broach the possibility of coming back the next day and taking a ride, given the cost. I remember Deb's words to the effect of "absolutely not" and "are you out of your mind?" I walked around for the next few minutes and then headed over to the trailer where the ground crew sold souvenirs. I made an appointment to fly the next day.

The ride in *Sentimental Journey* on July 16, 2006, fanned the flames ignited by the spark that touring the airplane the day before had struck. The indescribable pull of history, flight, and patriotism made the cost of a week's pay and my wife's disapproval seem like an insignificant price, certainly less than the price paid by the brave warriors who originally flew the aircraft. Being in that aircraft thousands of feet above the earth was like time traveling; I experienced a moment in the same physical surroundings as the airmen from years gone by.

That once-in-a-lifetime flight has resulted in this work and so much more. It has become part of, and continues to confirm, how I view the world and what I hold sacred. What follows is an account that did not begin or end with World War II, nor is it the complete story of all the sacrifices of Maine people. Maine has always had special everyday people who believed in freedom and put everything on the line to defend it. Maine is not alone. Citizens all over the United States could discover accounts like these hidden like gems in their own neighborhoods, if only they stopped and took the time to consider and mine the history that surrounds them.

Silent Maine Reminders is really only this man's recognition of some of Maine's history. It is only a few snapshots of who we are as a state and, ultimately, a nation. We only need to stop, open our eyes, listen with our ears, and appreciate with our hearts.

A park and a church in the center of town. (Photo by Alden Weigelt)

Chapter 2

A HOUSE AND A PARK IN THE CENTER OF TOWN

I grew up on Winter Street in Waterville, Maine. By the time I was born, my grandmother, Bessie B. Jackins, was my only surviving grandparent. My mother, my father, my brother Robert, and I lived upstairs in our section of the house, and my maternal grandmother and her daughter, my Aunt Marion, lived downstairs. The family business was the Preble Studio in Waterville. My parents and a friend of the family were partners in the business and Aunt Marion worked for them. The Preble Studio was a successful photography business and did sittings, weddings, and yearbook work. My mother was active in city politics for most of her life and served on the City Council, the Board of Aldermen, and the Board of Assessment Review. Needless to say, our family knew many people in the area.

Years before, during the Great Depression, my grandmother took in boarders, sewed for other people, and raised her three children. Her children worked to help the family, too. As a young girl, my mother (Myrtle) babysat and cleaned for a family in town. Aunt Marion babysat for families as well. Bessie's husband Alden, my grandfather for whom I was named, worked for the railroad. When he was later out of work, he did photo work and developing out of his home, as well as interior painting of homes for a paint store in town. His photo work was a home business and was not connected to the Preble Studio that my parents later owned and operated. They did whatever they could, as many other families did at that time, to make ends meet. They were known for their honesty and integrity and would accept no less from others. There were family stories of hunger, as well, that went hand-in-hand with an ethic of never turning a neighbor away.

My Aunt Marion's senior class trip was supposed to be to a camp on a lake a few miles out of town. However, due to the financial difficulties of the time, the school could afford neither a senior trip nor even a yearbook that year. That did not dampen the resolve or ingenuity of the senior class or the school staff. The school janitor loaned the kids his big open truck, the kids raised money for their own food, and the class went to the lake for their picnic. Aunt Marion told of her high school teachers at Waterville Senior High School: During the depression there wasn't enough money to pay them all, but many of them continued to teach just the same without being paid for several years. That's how strongly they believed in the importance and contribution of their calling.

As other commentators have noted, this was a different generation. The many that were out of work during that time felt ashamed of being without work, as if it was their fault. The shift today, it seems, is toward blaming the government and business with little regard for the power of the family and community to pull together when times get tough. I wonder, if this current recession were to worsen to the degree of the economic hardship of the thirties, would our generation have the guts to make it? And my answer is…I don't know.

Our house was centrally located in the city and was one street to the south of where Veterans Memorial Park stands today. When I was growing up, the park was known as Coburn Park, as it was adjacent to Coburn Classical Institute. Coburn was a private college preparatory school that existed in Waterville until merging with another private school, Oak Grove, in Vassalboro, in the early '70s. Coburn Park was eventually renamed Veterans Memorial Park years after the old school was torn down and replaced by a high-rise for the elderly.

Veterans Park, as it is known today, was appropriately named. It had first been known as the old cemetery on Elm Street, and had been a burial ground for Revolutionary War veterans for many years. Those graves were eventually relocated to the newer Pine Grove Cemetery in the south end of the city, and by the end of 1868, most of the bodies had been moved there. After the Civil War, in 1869, a statue of a Civil War soldier was erected on that ground as a memorial to those who had served in the war. The area was made a park and renamed Monument Square. Our family always referred to it as Monument Park.

In later years, the World War I Memorial, which lists the names of those who served and died in the Great War, was moved to Veterans Park from what had been known, until then, as Memorial Bridge. The

A lone sentinel in Waterville. (Photo by Alden Weigelt)

bridge crosses Messalonskee Stream on Kennedy Memorial Drive. Once improvements to the bridge were made, the World War I Memorial was moved. Then in 1999, the park was formally dedicated as Veterans Memorial Park in honor of all the area's war veterans.

Similar statues and memorials are a common sight in most Maine communities. Many of the statues located in the center of these towns are the same. The reason for this is simple, but often overlooked now. During the Civil War, there was a high ratio of soldiers to citizens from this state who went to serve in the Union Army. Based on this ratio, there were more men who went to war from Maine, based on population, than many of the other states. But when you look at the ratio of volunteers to draftees in the various state regiments that served in the war, the State of Maine holds the distinction of having the highest ratio of volunteers to draftees of any state in the Union. It is appropriate that our State Motto is "Dirigo," which means "I Lead."

While growing up in Waterville, every May there was a Memorial Day Parade. The remarks made in observance of that day were always made in Monument Park. The city used to erect a temporary reviewing stand for the dignitaries to speak from. There was always a reading of General Logan's Orders, which were the orders for the Grand Army of the Republic (GAR) to observe the decoration of the Civil War soldiers'

A lone sentinel in Winslow. (Photo by Alden Weigelt)

graves. There was also the reading of the Gettysburg Address and a gun salute and taps. When I was a kid, we were at war in Vietnam. It was the Army National Guard that provided the firing party for the gun salute at that time.

May 30th was originally designated as Decoration Day. This was the beginning of an observance that, in later years, became Memorial Day. Memorial Day was not started by the government or the thankful citizens of the Union that was saved. It was started by the veterans' organization of Civil War soldiers, the Grand Army of the Republic. It was started by veterans remembering their own. It did not become a national holiday until years later, and eventually the date was changed from May 30th to the last Monday of May by the government to facilitate a three-day weekend holiday. Sadly, many in our nation enjoy the long holiday weekend and the unofficial beginning of summer, but forget about the blood spilt that guaranteed their weekend.

The observance of Memorial Day in Veterans Park was something that my parents expected me to attend, and I was taught to do so in a respectful manner. When the remarks were made, I was taught to pay attention. There would be other kids waiting for the gun salute so they could rush over and pick up the spent cases. I made the mistake one year of joining in with them. My mother was quick to sharply correct me. This day was very important to my mother, as I will detail in later chapters. I attended the service with my parents until junior high school. At that time, I joined the school band and became part of the ceremony, playing with the band on Memorial Day throughout my junior high and high school years.

This is the park I played in as a kid. There are three Civil War naval cannons in the park. My friends and I used to pretend they were under our command. North of the park, on the corner of Elm and Park Streets, is the First Baptist Church. It is a massive white wooden structure even by today's standards. The church has stood there since 1826 and is the oldest surviving public building in Waterville.

In 1834, the church had a new minister by the name of Samuel Francis Smith. He received his ordination at the First Baptist Church. Two years earlier, while still in seminary, Smith had written the now famous anthem, "My Country, Tis of Thee," or "America," as it is also known. The words to the hymn are set to the tune of the British national anthem, "God Save the King." Smith claimed that he did not realize a connection to the British national anthem when he wrote the hymn.

This was the second time our two countries wrote beautiful music together. The first time occurred a few years earlier during a little quarrel we had in Chesapeake Bay with the British Royal Navy during the War of 1812. A lawyer by the name of Francis Scott Key jotted down his thoughts while watching the effect the British bombardment of 1814 had upon our flag, Fort McHenry, and ultimately our nation. It was many years after the words to the "Star-Spangled Banner" were written that it officially became our national anthem—117 years later, on March 3, 1931, to be exact. Until then, "My Country, 'Tis of Thee" was unofficially considered the national anthem and was one of our patriotic favorites during the Civil War.

Across Elm Street and east of the park is the Alvin Lombard house. Lombard earned a patent in 1901 for a steam-powered, tracked vehicle that hauled logs out of the forest. Lombard's invention was an early example of a practical application for the caterpillar tread. The caterpillar tread is now widely in use on construction and military vehicles all over the world.

We should also remember another famous inventor from Maine. Hiram Maxim was born in Sangerville, Maine. He is credited for inventing the machine gun, and his creation was soon in service around the world. His invention has been praised for its genius by some and cursed for its efficiency by others. I imagine that one's opinion would be influenced by which side of the weapon you're standing on. He is one of only

The old house on Winter Street. (Photo by Alden Weigelt)

two Mainers to date who has been knighted by the Sovereign of Great Britain.

Veterans Park is beautiful and central to the city. When I was a kid, there were several old men that spent hours on the park benches. Some were veterans, and sadly, some were also alcoholics. When I see the park today, I pause to wonder how many people passing through it or driving by it realize the significance of the sacrifices remembered there. How many look across the street to the beautiful church and realize how much history is there? How many other places of historical significance are enjoyed by citizens in other parts of our country with similar ignorance?

The house I grew up in on Winter Street looks out toward Veterans Park. Those who visited our home connected their history to ours, and our shared histories directly connected to the history of our nation. On Christmas 2010, I was reminded once again how powerfully people felt about that house on Winter Street and what it meant to them. Donna Pitts is a nurse and a member of Blessed Hope Church who has been a friend of the family associated with the house for about 12 years now. She presented the family with a poem she had written about her experiences visiting with them at 10 Winter Street.

Sacred

By Donna Pitts

Sunday at number ten.
Moments frozen in time,
On the walls, on the tables, in the frames.
God lingers here,
In the smiles, the laughter and the tears.
No pretense, no masks,
This is for real.
Comfort, sanctuary, hope.

Little ones, middle ones,
And the oldest of all.
Offerings of wisdom and faith.
Once is never enough,
Keep coming back for more.
Debates, soapbox speeches.
Integrity, honour, courage, truth, transparency,
And the greatest of these, is love.

Katahdin.
Need one say more?
Kayaks, guns, fishing poles.
Uniforms of warriors.
Never, ever forget!
Crock pots and pie plates.
The smells of coffee and a damn good cigar.
A nip or two here and there.

It is worship and it is prayer.
Take none of it lightly.
A family, truly rich beyond measure.
Many more memories ahead,
A new son has entered in.
But alas it's getting late,
Parting until next time,
Love you, see you.

Aunt Marion and Debora checking on Grampa in New Limerick, Maine.
(Photo by Alden Weigelt)

Chapter 3

A KIND OLD GENTLEMAN

On April 21, 2008, my wife and I visited the local cemetery in the small town of New Limerick, Maine, with Aunt Marion, who at the time was 90 years old. She showed us the headstone of her grandfather, John C. Bradbury, which declared "April 2, 1842 to June 2, 1931." We could tell by the stone and the one next to it that John was married twice. His first wife, Ella, died in 1879. His second wife, Ada, died in 1924.

Aunt Marion had been concerned about the condition of the stone, as it had been broken at least once in the past and repaired by her brother. She had last visited here over 20 years ago, and the stone had been broken again since then. We discovered that the stone had been repaired once more, and later learned of a local man who had taken the liberty of repairing several of the gravestones in the cemetery on his own and at his own expense. There was a "U.S. Veteran" flag holder stuck in the ground next to the headstone. Today, a second flag holder stands on the other side of his headstone. It states that the one buried there was a member of the Grand Army of the Republic.

John Cleaves Bradbury was born April 2, 1842, in Aroostook County, Maine. At the age of 19, he enlisted in the Regular Army in the 17th Regiment, United States Infantry at Fort Preble in South Portland, Maine, on March 8, 1862. The 17th U.S. Infantry trained at Fort Preble, and John was assigned to Company C, 1st Battalion. (The remains of the fort are now part of the Southern Maine Community College campus.) John had never been away from home before and came down with the measles during training. He was hospitalized at Fort Preble on May 1st. After being discharged from the hospital, John continued to train with his unit,

John C. Bradbury. (Photo by Alden Weigelt)

but on September 15th, he was hospitalized again, this time with typhoid fever.

After he was released from the hospital a second time, a weakened John continued to train with his unit. The 17th U.S. Infantry eventually left the state and headed south, arriving at and participating in the Battle of Fredericksburg that continued for three days, from December 12th through 15th. The South won the Battle of Fredericksburg. They were dug in to defend the city and repelled the attacks of the Northern infantry. During the 17th U.S. Infantry's history, it lost nine officers and 92 enlisted men in combat, and two officers and 100 enlisted men to disease.

In early January 1863, somewhere near Fredericksburg, John became sick again. This time he suffered from chronic diarrhea. The regimental surgeon sent John home to die. He told John that if he did not die on the trip home, he should have his mother churn fresh buttermilk for him every day. John survived the trip and his mother did as the surgeon had suggested. But this would not be the end of the story.

John was a Christian man. He read his Bible every day of his life. He did not drink alcohol, and all those who knew him loved him. John had five grandchildren, three girls and two boys. They knew that he was in

Joshua Lawrence Chamberlain Brunswick, Maine. (Photo by Alden Weigelt)

the Civil War and asked him about it, but he never told them about the fighting. When one granddaughter asked him why he had thrown his uniform away in the Potomac, he simply replied, "Because it was lousy." When another granddaughter asked why he had given the Confederates his food, he simply responded, "Because they were hungry." Mr. Bradbury drank hot water with a little milk and sugar in it six days a week. On Sundays, he added coffee. This was a reminder to him for the rest of his life of the shortage of coffee during the war and the other conditions he had endured while serving his country.

While John was home recovering from his near death due to the sickness he contracted after Fredericksburg, another God-fearing Mainer and veteran of Fredericksburg became the newly appointed colonel of the 20th Maine Volunteer Infantry Regiment or, as it is better known, the 20th Maine. Joshua Lawrence Chamberlain was a professor from Bowdoin College in Brunswick, Maine. He also survived the war and later became governor of Maine.

Chamberlain was in command of the 20th Maine when it became engaged at Gettysburg. On the second day of battle, on July 2, 1863, Chamberlain was ordered to hold the extreme left of the Union Army on a rocky hill known as Little Round Top.

The position that the 20th held was crucial. If they lost the ground, the Confederates would own the high ground on the Union left flank, and if they got their artillery in place, they would be able to rake the Union line for more than a mile. It was very likely the Union Army would lose the day if that happened, and history now tells us it could have meant losing the war. In hindsight, the Union victory at Gettysburg is seen as the turning point in the Civil War. The Union had very few victories in the war until those three days in July of 1863. The battle at Gettysburg had a huge cost for both sides, with combined casualties of 48,040.

The 2nd of July was very hot, as you can imagine Pennsylvania is at that time of year. The 20th was opposite the 15th Alabama Infantry. The Alabamians outnumbered the 20th more than two to one, and attacked again and again up the hill. The 20th held, but in doing so allowed the line to double back on itself. Imagine one part of the line being a wall, and the other part of the line being a door. As the Alabamians attacked, the door part of the 20th's line swung back until it was almost touching the wall portion of the line. At the apex of the now bent line stood Colonel Chamberlain, the Colors of the United States of America, and the Battle Colors of the 20th Maine.

When Francis Scott Key wrote the words to the "Star-Spangled Banner" in 1814, our flag had 15 stars representing the 15 states at the time. On July 2, 1863, our flag had 34 stars representing all the states at the time, including North and South. The union of all the states, both North and South, was what the Union Army was so desperately trying to preserve. The Confederate flag that had repeatedly charged up the hill that day was known as the Stars and Bars. It had only 13 stars representing the 13 states that were fighting to leave the Union. And the determined men charging with it believed in their cause, too.

And then the 20th began to run out of ammunition. They had men down and they had lost much of their strength. All was at stake. If the 20th Maine failed in its mission, the day would be lost.

So Chamberlain gave the first of the two commands in his life that he would go down in history for. The first was in preparation for the destruction of an enemy that was trying to destroy the Union, which he and the farmers and fishermen from Maine beside him believed in. Not only did the Alabamians vastly outnumber them, but Chamberlain's troops had exhausted their own ammunition. Chamberlain, himself wounded, gave the order: "BAYONET!" As one unit, the 20th drew their bayonets and, with the "clatter of metal upon metal," affixed them to their rifles. What followed was the sound of their cheers as they prepared to do what they had come to do this day. The outnumbered men from Maine executed a closing of the door portion of the line in a "right wheel" maneuver, and then charged down the hill. The startled Confederates broke and ran. The

20th killed or captured most of the remainder of the men from Alabama. Joshua Chamberlain received the Congressional Medal of Honor in recognition of his leadership and bravery that day. He was later promoted to brigadier general. In March of 1865, Chamberlain was promoted to brevet major general by Abraham Lincoln. Chamberlain was to survive the war after being more seriously wounded two more times.

The war was not over for John C. Bradbury, however. In October of 1864, the Union Army was in so much need of men that a draft was put in place. John had enlisted in the 17th U.S. Infantry as a volunteer before the draft. He had already served and was now exempt, as he had been discharged for medical reasons. But when John was drafted, he never acknowledged that he had already served and been discharged. John went back, this time as a draftee, into the 16th Regiment, Maine Infantry. During the entire history of the 16th Maine, it lost a total of nine officers and 172 enlisted men in combat and two officers and 257 enlisted men to disease.

Once the Union Army figured out that John had a prior service history, he was given the task of drill instructor. He drilled the new recruits and helped square them away. He was later assigned to the Provost Guard in the Headquarters Company of the 16th Maine. Again, he never spoke of the engagements he was in, but his granddaughters knew he had fought at Fredericksburg, Five Forks and Appomattox Courthouse. It was there, at Appomattox, that he witnessed Lee's surrender and witnessed and responded to the second historical command that Brevet Major General Joshua Lawrence Chamberlain would issue.

In April of 1865, the Union troops and the Army of Northern Virginia were once again opposite each other. On the morning of April 9th, they fought a final battle at Appomattox Courthouse. Lee soon realized that the South could not go on, and it was decided that Lee would surrender to the Union. Later on the same afternoon, Palm Sunday, April 9, 1865, General Robert E. Lee met General Ulysses S. Grant in a small house at Appomattox Courthouse. After terms were agreed upon and the surrender was signed, it was decided that the Confederate troops would come into Appomattox on a later date to surrender their arms and colors. Under the terms of the surrender, the Confederate officers were allowed to retain their sidearms. All soldiers using their own horses were allowed to take the animals home in order to facilitate plowing and the growing of crops. While waiting for this day to come, the armies camped opposite each other. The Confederates were starving, and many of the Union troops, including John Bradbury, shared with the Confederate soldiers the little food they had.

On April 12, 1865, Bvt. Maj. General Chamberlain was given the honor of receiving the formal surrender of the Army of Northern Virginia as they came to surrender their colors and arms. John C. Bradbury described to his grandchildren his eyewitness account of this event, but never the details of the battles.

The Union troops had been assembled in formation with Chamberlain in command. What happened next had been carefully thought out by the general. Chamberlain observed Confederate General John B. Gordon leading the column of marching men on horseback, and later recalled that the general looked very dejected and seemed to slump on his horse. As General Gordon approached, Chamberlain called his own troops to "CARRY ARMS." This was not the "present arms" salute, at that time only issued as the highest honor, but rather, as Chamberlain explained, it was the marching salute and an honor given to other soldiers. Gordon was startled by the "machine-like, sudden shift of arms" and recognized immediately what was happening. Chamberlain later remarked that General Gordon recovered his attitude as a soldier. Gordon gently touched his horse with his spur, and horse and rider wheeled toward Chamberlain. The horse slightly bowed as Gordon touched the point of his saber to his right stirrup in salute to General Chamberlain. General Gordon then ordered his own troops to "CARRY ARMS" and the Confederates returned the honor.

The Confederates continued to march into Appomattox Courthouse, and more than 27,000 men in gray surrendered arms that day. Many wept over the colors that they now laid down. The Union troops were silent and there was no cheering the surrender or the defeat of their enemy. It was said that many Union cheeks were wet as well. The Civil War would soon be over, and Joshua Chamberlain had made the first gesture toward healing a tattered nation by extending respect to the men who would now become brother Americans again. Two days later, on Good Friday, April 14, 1865, Abraham Lincoln, the President of the United States, was shot by an assassin. The next day he was dead.

John C. Bradbury was transferred into the 20th Maine as the numbers of the 16th Maine were combined with the numbers of the 20th. He marched in the Grand Review of the Union Army in Washington, D.C., after Lincoln's death. His discharge from the Army of the Potomac was from the storied 20th Maine.

In later years, John Bradbury did respond to an inquiry that his daughter Bessie (Bradbury) Jackins made in regard to his service. Bessie was considering joining the Daughters of the American Revolution, and evidently, John's service in the Union Army during the Civil War would be meaningful in her application. John's reply was typical of his humble character. After briefly providing her the dates and units that he was assigned to, he wrote: "I did not do anything to distinguish myself, just a private soldier, nothing more." He signed the letter: "Your Obedient Father, John C. Bradbury." We know, of course, that this was not true. In fact, John had distinguished himself in many ways, including going back and serving a second time when he did not have to. He survived sickness then combat, sickness again, and combat once more.

John continued to distinguish himself by his character for the rest of his life. He had two experiences with losing his property to fire. When his farmhouse burned down in Weeks Mills, he wrote his daughter a postcard. He simply stated, "The house burned down last night, I didn't." Years before, a relative had given John the bad news in dramatic fashion that his mill had burned down. John's reply was, "Oh, is that all? I thought someone had died."

After the death of his second wife, John lived at the house on Winter Street with his daughter Bessie, her husband Alden, and their three children, Prescott, Myrtle and Marion. The children loved and adored their grandfather.

John C. Bradbury outlived two wives. He died three days after Decoration Day, on June 2, 1931, at 89 years of age at the old Thayer Hospital on Main Street in Waterville. John's wake was at that old house on Winter Street at the home of his family. Friends came to call and showed their deepest respect. His body was escorted by Bessie Bradbury Jackins, his daughter by his second wife, to New Limerick, Maine by train. It was there he was laid to rest in the Bradbury section of the cemetery. Veterans of the World War acted as bearers and he was buried with full military honors.

The papers reported that John had the distinction of being the only Maine soldier, if not the only Union Army soldier, to be both a volunteer and a draftee. John was a life member of the Grand Army of the Republic and had five grandchildren that he adored. John was loved by all who knew him and would be remembered as a kind old gentleman.

There exists a photo of the Civil War Monument in Winslow with nine old Civil War veterans in front of it. The date is either 1929 or 1930, from the age of the automobile in the background, and it was probably taken on Decoration Day (Memorial Day). John Bradbury is third from the left. He is ramrod straight and his hat is squarely on his head, and he is looking the camera directly in the lens. John is either 87 or 88 years old in this photograph. The kind old gentleman was also…a warrior.

John is third from the left. He is ramrod straight and his hat is squarely on his head. John is looking the camera directly in the lens. The old gentleman was also…a warrior. (Photo courtesy of Marion Jackins)

Chapter 4

A FEW MEN AND FATHERS OF WATERVILLE

One of my favorite movies of all time is the 1946 film, *The Best Years of Our Lives.* In 1947, it received eight Academy Awards, including Best Picture. The story is about three veterans returning from World War II to a fictitious small town. The picture illustrates for the audience some of the real struggles men who had just returned from war faced at the time. The story continues to tell how each of the three men starts over as a civilian after experiencing a war that changed them for the rest of their lives.

The film goes on to show that most of those at home don't really understand the change in their friend or loved one, and wonder why they just can't flip a switch and immediately be their old self again. But the veterans need to heal from their experiences in their own ways. The ones who are patient and truly understand them are few, but, as is true in reality, those who *are* patient will earn the veterans' love and appreciation for the rest of their lives. Maybe some of the guys mentioned in Chapter 1 kept coming back to Winter Street for that very same reason.

Eventually, most got on with life in the civilian world, and many raised families. They went about their lives, and most around them forgot the little that they knew about what their friend or loved one did in the war. But those who experience war never forget it. They live with it every day. If they speak of it at all, it is most likely to another with similar service experiences. Even the closest family members may be considered outsiders regarding some of these memories.

Jimmy Stewart, the famous actor, was a bomber pilot in the 8th Air

Force based in England during World War II. Stewart flew combat missions against Germany from there. He was a humble and shy man. He entered the army as a private in March of 1941, about nine months before the United States got into the war, and shortly after receiving an Academy Award for Best Actor for his performance in *The Philadelphia Story*. Earlier, Stewart had received a Best Actor nomination for his performance in the 1939 film, *Mr. Smith Goes to Washington*. Despite his successful acting career, Stewart was determined to serve his country.

Stewart knew it was just a matter of time before we got into this war, and he was not an isolationist, as so many other Americans were at the time. However, he was not initially accepted into the army. He was too thin, being ten pounds too light. After reapplying, he was finally accepted. Stewart was an accomplished private pilot with over three hundred flying hours. He wanted to fly for his country, but at the time could only enter the military as an enlisted man and a private.

Stewart finally got his wish. The army trained him to fly bombers, and then made him an instructor pilot who taught other young men how to fly them. But Stewart wasn't satisfied; he wanted to fly bombers in combat. The army was reluctant to send him into harm's way due to his fame. They were also concerned about what it might do to the morale of the nation and for the morale of the enemy if he were killed or captured. Stewart persisted, and eventually went to England as a bomber pilot. He came home a full bird colonel and wing commander.

For his service during World War II, Colonel James Maitland Stewart received the Distinguished Flying Cross with Oak Leaf Cluster for his performance in the 8th Air Force, meaning Jimmy twice received one of the nation's highest decorations for heroism. The 8th Air Force is also fondly known as the Mighty Eighth Air Force to its members. Jimmy stayed in the Air Force Reserve after the war and retired a brigadier general.

General Stewart once told a reporter in an interview that he thought about his military career every day. He considered it one of the great experiences of his life. The reporter asked if it was greater than his movie career, and he answered that it was "much greater."

As I mentioned in Chapter 2, most of my friends while growing up had a parent who served somehow during World War II. Lee Cabana's dad, also named Lee, served in the Pacific Theater as an officer in the army and would later retire from the Maine Army National Guard as a lieutenant colonel. In his civilian job, he worked for the post office, and later helped start a church credit union.

Chris, Elaine, and Steve Libby's dad, George Libby, served on the navy destroyer escort USS *Robert E. Peary* (DE-132). The *Peary* provided

Larry LaMarre (Photo courtesy of Kevin LaMarre and Tia LaMarre Dupler)

convoy escort in the Atlantic. When George returned home, he worked as a self-employed TV repairman and owned his own shop in the early days of television. When the TVs got more dependable and the service calls fewer, he and his sons picked up the *Morning Sentinel* paper bundles at the newspaper print shop and delivered them all around Central Maine.

Kevin and Tia LaMarre's dad served in the navy in the Pacific Theater. Larry LaMarre was also a Pearl Harbor survivor, and he worked the rest of his life as an electrician, eventually becoming the electrical supervisor at Scott Paper Company in Winslow. Larry was near the submarine docks the morning of Sunday, December 7, 1941, when the Japanese bombed Pearl Harbor. He had a front-row seat. He was able to clearly recognize the pilots as Japanese, as they flew by so closely. Larry was a newly trained navy diver at the time. After the bombing, he used his new diving skills in the aftermath to help recover bodies from the attacked ships. Larry LaMarre never told his children the details of what must have been a horrific task.

Larry also served on the cruiser USS *Minneapolis* (CA-36) during the Battle of the Coral Sea. Later in the war, he trained in underwater demolition, and before we landed our marines on Guadalcanal, Larry was there. These guys were the forerunners of the Navy SEALS of today. His team was there to locate, clear, and designate the landing areas for the marines. They did this at night, and by day hid in the banyan trees. He later explained to his son that the Japanese troops were at times so close that he could have reached out and touched them.

At one point in his service, Larry was wounded in combat by shrapnel. Larry's son, Kevin, remembered that his Dad never spoke of these things at great length, and it was over a period of forty-plus years, and in little bits and pieces, that Kevin gathered this information from his dad. Kevin recalled thinking that this was very typical of his dad's generation. This was not a generation obsessed with self, but a generation that grew up with very little, and then laid that little on the line for the freedom of the world. Larry LaMarre continued his service in the Naval Reserve through the Korean War. Kevin also remembered that his dad always referred to the Japanese soldiers as the "Japanese boys." He never heard his father refer to them as "Nips" or "Japs."

And these were just a few. I remember several other fathers of friends, but did not know which branch of service they served in, and there were many.

Frank Siviski was the leader of Boy Scout Troop 412 of Sacred Heart Church. I was just starting in scouting when Frank was the leader. When he stepped down, he still participated with the other fathers in helping with the troop. Frank was a navy veteran, having served aboard the aircraft carrier USS *Monterey* (CVL-26). A young naval officer by the name of Gerald Ford was serving on board, as well. Frank recalled in later years knowing the young man that would someday be president of the United States. Like Larry LaMarre, Frank raised a family and worked for Scott Paper Company for the rest of his life.

Waterville High School's Ancient History teacher, Stetson Beal, was a naval officer and pilot. As I remember, Stet flew the PBY Catalina and dropped depth charges on enemy subs in combat. He was also my Driver's Ed teacher. When he found out that I was interested in aviation, he was excited about it and was a great encouragement to me over the years.

My flight instructor, John B. Gibbons, was a navy submarine veteran who served in the Pacific on subs during World War II. I believe it was not until after he served his 20 years that he took up flying. He used to joke about his time under the water and his time in the air being in competition with his time on the surface of the earth. When I met him, he had just retired as an airline pilot, but continued to fly by instructing students and doing charter work. John had several thousand flying hours when I met him in 1973. He was the manager of Waterville's Robert LaFleur Municipal Airport for several years, and lived with his wife, Christine, on the field. John's hobby was working on his model railroad. He was fascinated with it.

After John retired, he moved to Portsmouth, New Hampshire, closer to his naval roots and their veteran services. Deb and I would stop by to see him from time to time, and we introduced him to our kids. The last time I saw him was at my home. He dropped in to see us, and, by coincidence, I was in the process of building a model railroad for my son. I mentioned in Chapter 1 that the sense of smell is a strong memory producer. John Gibbons loved to smoke his pipe and would do so while flying, as well as when giving a flying lesson. Whenever I smell a pipe now, I think of him and airplanes.

These men came home from war and got on with their civilian lives, and, for most, with the job of raising a family. I remember these men as great guys who loved their kids and worked hard at providing for them. And like the rest, they had both similar and very different memories of their war experiences, as well as, I imagine, similar struggles while reentering civilian life. And like General James Maitland Stewart, they would remember their service for the rest of their lives. They are all dead now, but I will remember them for the rest of *my* life.

Waterville, ME 04901 the Old Post Office. (Photo by Alden Weigelt)

Chapter 5

UNITED STATES POST OFFICE, WATERVILLE, ME 04901

Just down the street from the First Baptist Church and the little park in the center of Waterville is another landmark, Post Office Square. The square is at the meeting of Upper Main Street, College Avenue, Lower Main Street, and Elm Street. All four streets merge and cross at this point to form an "X." Upper Main Street turns into Lower Main Street heading south, and Elm Street turns into College Avenue heading north.

Where College Avenue begins heading north sits the Waterville Fire Station. At the apex where Elm Street ends and Lower Main Street begins is a triangle of land that makes up the grounds of the old post office. The old post office building still stands here, but the post office itself was moved about a half mile up College Avenue in 1976. The old post office was in service between 1911 and 1976, and on the Main Street side of the building, on the basement level, were the local armed forces recruiting offices. The entrance to the basement on that side of the building was at street level. I remember the recruiting signs that used to be set out each day on the sidewalk in a metal frame, advertising the different branches of service, each in seeming competition with the other.

Right across the street from the recruiting office was the first pizza shop in town, Whipper's Pizza. The shop was in a very small brick building, no bigger than a medium-sized kitchen of the time. I didn't like pizza as a kid, and it wasn't until I was an adult that I learned to like it.

Waterville was home to two colleges when I was growing up. Thomas College was a business college located on Silver Street at the other end of town. These buildings became the home of the Maine Criminal Justice Academy when Thomas College moved to the West River Road. The Criminal Justice Academy trained all law enforcement officers in the State of Maine at this location until the state located a much-needed larger site in Vassalboro—the home of the former Oak Grove-Coburn School that I mentioned earlier in this book.

The other college in town was Colby College, which is now a leading liberal arts college. Colby was originally founded by Baptists in 1813 as the Maine Literary and Theological Institution. In 1821, it was renamed Waterville College. The original location of Waterville College, and subsequently Colby College, was on College Avenue about six-tenths of a mile up the road from Post Office Square.

During the Civil War, Waterville College was almost closed because so many of the students were away fighting for the Union. A Baptist philanthropist by the name of Gardner Colby made a large donation to the school to allow it to stay open, so it was later renamed Colby College in gratitude to Mr. Colby. Years later, in the 1930s, Colby relocated to its present campus on Mayflower Hill.

At this time, we should again remember Rev. Samuel Francis Smith of the Waterville Baptist Church. Rev. Smith not only served as pastor of the church and had written "My Country, 'Tis of Thee," but he was also the professor of modern languages at Waterville College. In 1869, at the old Colby campus on College Avenue, Memorial Hall was dedicated. It was the first Civil War memorial erected on a college campus, and it was dedicated to the Colby College men who had died in that war. In addition to being a memorial, it was also the library and chapel of the college.

After the college was relocated to Mayflower Hill, the old buildings on College Avenue remained unused and fell into disrepair for several years, Memorial Hall among them. George Libby, mentioned in the last chapter, and my mother were among several citizens of Waterville who attempted to save the building for its historical significance and in tribute to those Civil War soldiers who left their school, went to war, and died in the prime of their lives. Twenty Colby College men lost their lives fighting for the Union and the ultimate freedom of their fellow man. Unfortunately, my mother's and Mr. Libby's attempts to save the building proved unsuccessful.

The old Memorial Hall was abandoned and torn down in 1969, and this Silent Maine Reminder no longer exists. But there was something of significance salvaged from the library of Memorial Hall and moved to Miller Library at the new campus on the hill in 1962. It is a sculpture and tablet. The sculpture is known as the *Weeping Lion* and is based on the

The Weeping Lion and twenty brave Colby men. (Photo by Alden Weigelt. Printed by permission of Colby College)

Lion of Lucerne by Thorvaldsen. The *Weeping Lion* was created by Martin Millmore of Boston. The lion is depicted in the agony of death, dealt by the piercing of a spear. The lion lies on the Shield of the United States, protecting it while dying. The tablet bears the names of the twenty Colby men who died for the Union. The *Weeping Lion* was originally dedicated at Memorial Hall in 1871. I hope that all Colby students today realize and recognize the true cost of their education when they pass this tribute in the hall of their library.

In May of 1970, I was finishing up my year in the eighth grade at Waterville Junior High School on Gilman Street. The late '60s and the early '70s were a time of turmoil for our country and for Maine due to the opposition to our involvement in the war in Vietnam. Across the nation, college students were protesting the war, the draft, and many ROTC programs on their various campuses.

On May 4, 1970, at Kent State University in Ohio, four students were killed and nine others wounded during a protest rally when Army

National Guard soldiers opened fire in the direction of student demonstrators. Not all of those injured or killed were actively demonstrating at the time, and the nation was stunned.

The *Colby Echo* date accounts of what occurred in Waterville after the Kent State incident are conflicted. The *Colby Echo* article, in the issue of May 8, 1970, lists the day as May 5th. A follow-up article in the issue of February 20, 2003, lists the day as May 6th. My recollection of the incident is consistent with the 1970 *Echo* article with the following events occurring on May 5, 1970.

I was walking with my friend, Kevin LaMarre, near the junior high school on Gilman Street. It was a beautiful spring day, warm and sunny. We saw a large group of college students silently marching down Gilman Street from the direction of Colby College on Mayflower Hill. They were marching toward the center of town. There must have been at least four hundred of them. Some convertible automobiles were part of the procession, with makeshift coffins on the rear of each. One student beat a bass drum in the somber parade. There were four coffins in all, which we later learned represented the four killed at Kent State just the day before. The demonstration was escorted by a Waterville Police Department cruiser, and the march appeared peaceful as well as being sanctioned by the city.

Curious, we followed the demonstration. Kevin's dad was the Larry LaMarre mentioned in the previous chapter. Kevin's family and my family were both supporters of the U.S. efforts in Vietnam at the time, and we did not approve of the position of the antiwar demonstrators. We were, however, saddened by the Kent State incident.

The marchers ultimately arrived at Post Office Square. Kevin and I walked across the street to watch and stood in front of Whipper's Pizza. The coffins were deposited on the lawn of the post office. The postal workers had come out to stand on the front steps, and by the look of the postal workers, we knew that the demonstration would not be allowed to enter the post office without some opposition. You see, the majority of the postal workers were World War II veterans, and it was obvious by their expressions that they did not support the demonstrators.

A student leader of the demonstration spoke to the crowd on a handheld public address system. Kevin and I had left the area in front of Whipper's by this time to stand with the postal workers on the front steps of their post office. The student concluded his remarks and then approached the flagpole on the plaza of the post office, where he and another student began to lower the American flag to half-staff.

The flag of the United States now had grown to fifty stars, and the 1st Amendment of our Constitution guarantees each citizen of each state the free speech that had just been exercised that day. However, in regard to the flag, it is not to be flown at half-staff unless so ordered by the president of the United States or the governor of the state that the flag is flown in. The postal workers on the steps understood this; many had fought and knew many others who had died to preserve this sacred freedom. They had listened quietly and respectfully while the student spoke, but now, with the students' action to lower the flag, they were enraged.

Time seemed to slow. The postal workers stormed off the steps toward the flagpole and the two students engaged in lowering the flag from full to half-staff. One postal worker had to be held back by two others, as I am sure an assault would have occurred. Several of the students who had been quiet and respectful during the demonstration suddenly charged forward. Kevin and I approached in support of the postal workers. The *Colby Echo* article from May 8, 1970, reported that Postmaster Louis P. L. Loubier informed the protestors that, as the official in charge of a federal building, he had the authority to call out the National Guard.

I only remember seeing one Waterville policeman on scene during the incident. There may have been others, but I only remember one. I assume that he had been the officer escorting the demonstration. The officer immediately walked forward and ordered the opposing factions to disengage. Then he explained to the Colby students that their right to demonstrate did not include touching the post office flag. The officer also persuaded the angry postal workers to back off.

The police officer took the halyard of the flag away from those who were fighting to control it. He began to raise the flag and was relieved by a postal worker who finished the job. The postal worker tied the knot of the halyard after the flag of the United States of America had been restored to its proper display.

The Waterville officer acted with respect, calm, and quiet determination. Both sides knew better than to interfere with him. The Waterville police officer believed in the Constitution of the United States and knew the rules about respecting our country's flag.

The *Colby Echo* article of May 8, 1970, said that while the flag was being restored to full staff, the "crowd clapped rhythmically: one student shouted 'Pig!'" The *Echo* article gave credit to the police by saying that they "maintained order by acting in a friendly manner toward the crowd." The *Waterville Morning Sentinel* of May 6, 1970, article covering the demonstration reported Postmaster Loubier's actions and also gave credit to the police. The article states that "Waterville Police were thanked by Postmaster Louis P. L. Loubier for the combination of restraint and efficiency which they displayed."

The students from Colby, whose alumni had so much history during the Civil War, packed up their demonstration and went back to their college on the hill. At least one young female demonstrator was seen wrapped in a different American flag.

Chapter 6

PRINCETON VOR 1430 HRS., JANUARY 24, 1963

In January of 1963, most of the Colby College students in the demonstration that Kevin LaMarre and I witnessed at Post Office Square in 1970 were in junior high or early high school. They were about the same age as Kevin and I were when we witnessed their response to the Kent State tragedy that May. In 1963, the United States was in the middle of the Cold War. The Soviets were hell-bent on spreading communism around the globe, and the United States and her allies were just as determined to prevent it. This did not give rise to a lot of trust between the Soviets and NATO, and, as Winston Churchill had so eloquently stated in March of 1946 at Westminster College in Fulton, Missouri, an "Iron Curtain" had descended between the East and the West.

The Second World War had been fought at the cost of 72 million lives worldwide. Korea had cost the United States a little over 54,000 lives, and in the few short years to come, Vietnam would cost the United States over 58,000 lives. In contrast, 100 years earlier, during only three days in July of 1863, just a little over 48,000 Americans had met their end in a single battle outside a little Pennsylvania town by the name of Gettysburg.

In 1963, however, the concern was more ominous than an isolated battle or war in some foreign land. The very real concern hung on the prospect of the total destruction of the United States and ultimately, the world. Mankind had discovered fission, and the only two nuclear weapons that were ever used in warfare had been dropped on Japan in August of 1945. The energy released came from a chain reaction of atoms splitting and then bombarding and splitting more atoms. We had killed more Japanese during the conventional firebombing raids leading up to the two atomic raids, but this had required hundreds of aircraft and thousands of personnel. The two atomic raids demonstrated what just one aircraft and crew could do. Imagine hundreds of aircraft armed with nuclear weapons.

And then the weapon evolved.

In 1963, fission weapons were already old news. Fusion was here to stay. The first fusion bomb, or hydrogen bomb, was about five hundred times more powerful than the first bomb that we dropped on Hiroshima, Japan. The fission (atomic) bombs split the atom to release energy in a chain reaction. The fusion (hydrogen) bomb fuses, or combines, atoms in a chain reaction, and through physics produces a much higher yield of energy. To put it in perspective, a hydrogen bomb uses an atomic bomb as the triggering device.

And here is the complication of 1963. May I remind you that the Soviets had hydrogen bombs, too, and the Soviets were not really our friends. Strategic bombing, which included the bombing of civilians, had been widely used by both sides in the Second World War and there was fear it would be used again.

I started grammar school at North Grammar, located at the intersections of Pleasant and North Streets in Waterville. After I completed the first grade, North Grammar closed. The city had a new high school, and the old high school on Gilman Street became the junior high school, while the old junior high school on Pleasant Street reverted to a grammar school, becoming the Pleasant Street School. Today, it is known as the Albert S. Hall School in honor of Albert Hall, a former superintendent of the Waterville school system and husband to my former kindergarten teacher, Marilyn Hall. (Mrs. Hall was also the subject of my very first crush.) I began second grade at Pleasant Street School in the fall of 1963.

While still at North Grammar, I remember an incident that should be mentioned at this time. We used to have fire drills all the time at school. I remember, however, a very different kind of drill, but I don't believe all the other students had the same understanding of the drill as I did. This was around the time of the Cuban Missile Crisis.

There was a siren outside the school building, and the siren was different from the kind that one heard coming from a police or fire vehicle of the time. The tone did not fluctuate and was a steady wail. The different siren sounded that day, and the fire bell in the school rang in a different sequence than it did for the regular fire drill. Instead of evacuating the school, we were led to the lower corridors of the building. We, being the younger children, were directed to lean against the walls on both sides of the corridors with our arms up around our heads. Then the children from the older grades came downstairs and assumed the same position, leaning over the younger children.

I heard another student ask a girl who was the same age as me, why we were not going outside like we did during a normal fire drill, and why we were hiding our eyes. The girl responded that she thought it was so we wouldn't see the fire. This drill had never been explained as being different from a fire drill. My parents had explained the difference in the type of drills to me, but I still wonder how many other children were encouraged from such drills, with lack of explanation, to hide under their bed or in a closet from a real fire.

In January 1963, it was believed that the only deterrent to a Soviet nuclear first strike on the United States was a response in kind to their attack with just as much destructive power. The concept of mutually assured destruction (MAD) would, hopefully, deter an aggressor from launching a first strike because it meant *his* total destruction as well. The only problem was making sure that we could successfully respond to the other guy with a retaliatory strike of our own. This involves having enough strike capability left after being attacked first, as well as being able to deliver that strike capability to the other guy.

One of our primary nuclear payload delivery systems at the time was the bomber, and the primary strategic bomber then was the Boeing B-52 Stratofortress. The B-52 entered operational service in 1954. The B-52 is still going strong today, and is projected to continue in service until 2040, an impressive 86 years. The B-52 has been affectionately referred to by her aircrews as the "BUFF" (Big Ugly Fat F**ker). For the gentle and polite members of society among us (Big Ugly Fat Fellow) works just as well in substitution.

In 1963, the Strategic Air Command (SAC) was in charge of the air force's nuclear arsenal, including bombers and Intercontinental Ballistic Missiles (ICBMs). After the collapse of the Soviet Union, the air force went through a reorganization, and in 1992, SAC was disbanded. For the first time since their introduction, there were no longer nuclear-armed B-52s airborne around the clock, seven days a week. The motto of SAC was "Peace is our Profession." And SAC lived up to its motto, as we are all still here.

The B-52 had been designed for high-level strategic bombing, primarily with a nuclear payload. It was also to prove itself efficient as a conventional bomber, delivering conventional munitions during later conflicts. In the early '60s, the Soviets got good at high-altitude air defense with their radar-guided surface-to-air missiles (SAMs). If we were to be able to offer a deterrent through MAD, we had to find a way to get our bombers through.

Maine had two SAC bases at the time, Dow Air Force Base (AFB) in Bangor and Loring AFB in Limestone. In Portsmouth, New Hampshire, was Pease AFB (also part of SAC), and historically, their unit had descended from the bomb group that had dropped the atomic bombs, Little Boy and Fat Man, on Japan. All three of these bases supported the nuclear mission of the B-52. If you think that the little old State of Maine was a safe place to be during the Cold War, think again. These bases were definitely near the top of the list of primary targets for the Soviets to destroy.

On January 24, 1963, at about 1430 Hrs., a B-52C, Tail Number 53-0406, passed over the Princeton VOR (VOR stands for VHF Omni Range and is a radio navigation aid for aircraft) and descended to 500 feet above ground level (AGL). It began a low-level attack profile in a simulated attempt to fly in under enemy radar at 280 knots (about 322 mph). This was the first low-level terrain-avoidance navigation training exercise to take place on the East Coast. The flight route was on the training route designated POKER DECK 8-3 in Maine. The crew had been given the choice of flying POKER DECK 8-3, a northern training route, or POKER DECK 8-5, a southern training route in the Carolinas. The crew had chosen the northern route after considering the current weather information.

The B-52 had been designed for high-altitude attack, but this day was testing new terrain-following radar in an attempt to defeat the new Soviet air defenses, which it would face at normal altitude. The aircraft, flying out of the Westover SAC base in Massachusetts, was not armed at the time. The bomber was rigged for the test, and there were nine crewmembers aboard, three more than the standard six that comprised a combat crew, due to the test. The call sign given to Tail Number 53-0406 for that day's mission was "FROSH 10."

About 21 minutes after passing Princeton VOR, at about 1451 Hrs., Tail Number 53-0406 encountered turbulence in the vicinity of Elephant Mountain, just outside of Greenville. The aircraft commander began a climb above it. There came a loud noise and the aircraft rolled into a sharp right bank and began to descend. Though the crew did not know it at the time, the vertical stabilizer of the aircraft had snapped off.

The aircraft commander was unable to gain control, and seconds later ordered that the aircraft be abandoned. At each crew station is a warning light that illuminates if the aircraft commander orders the abandonment of the aircraft. When I interviewed him on March 22, 2011, navigator Captain Gerald J. Adler, who was flying in the electronic warfare officer (EWO) position of the aircraft, told me that the "abandon aircraft" warning light came on, and then his watch stopped at 1452 Hrs.

In memory of Tail Number 53-0406. (Photo by Alden Weigelt)

Chapter 7

LOST THEN FOUND IN GREENVILLE, MAINE

Staff Sergeant William Lindie was just about to get off work on January 24, 1963, at the Security Police K-9 Sentry Dog Section of Dow AFB in Bangor. The Sentry Dog Headquarters Section was near the nuclear weapons storage area, across I-95 and southwest of the base in Hampden. SSgt. Lindie was the assistant non-commissioned officer in charge (NCOIC) of the Air Force Security Police K-9 Sentry Dog Force at Dow, and was also on the base's search and rescue team. SSgt. Lindie had been notified of the B-52 crash and ordered to Greenville that evening. The sergeant knew that he would need personal equipment in addition to what he had at the base, and quickly headed home to Winslow to gather it. He then headed for Greenville.

The responding air force personnel were billeted in the gym at Greenville High School. That night, it was still not known by the responders whether Tail Number 53-0406 had been carrying a standard combat load of two hydrogen bombs, as many times training missions were armed in case the order to go to war came in the middle of a training exercise. If the bomber were armed, that meant the responding teams were responding to what is known by the code phrase "Broken Arrow," meaning that a nuclear weapon accident had occurred, and specifically, in this case, that the release of nuclear radiation was possible. SSgt Lindie and his team were trained for this possibility.

The next morning, after roll call at 0700 Hrs., assignments were made to the teams. It was now known that Tail Number 53-0406 had *not* been armed with nuclear weapons, and that there had been nine souls on board, an additional three due to the training mission, as well as classified data and equipment. The first priority was to rescue any survivors.

In civilian aviation the pilot flies in command of the aircraft in the left seat and the copilot assists the pilot from the right seat. In the military the terms are a little different but the roles are the same. The normal configuration of a B-52 includes the aircraft commander in the left seat, the pilot (copilot in civilian speak) in the right seat, and the EWO behind the aircraft commander on the left side of the aircraft on the flight deck. Captain Gerald Adler was a navigator, but was flying in the EWO position on the flight deck at this time in the mission. All three positions on the flight deck are equipped with an ejection seat that ejects the crewmember straight up through the top of the aircraft.

Below the flight deck are the navigator and radar navigator positions, and those crewmembers eject straight down out of the bottom of the aircraft. There is a tail gunner in the tail of the aircraft, and the person in that position does not eject, but jettisons the gun turret, comprised of four .50-caliber machine guns, and then bails out of the space where the guns were. Any other persons on the aircraft would bail out through the holes left by the navigator and radar navigator after they "eject," or through the entry door in the bottom of the aircraft.

Another navigator was below the flight deck in Captain Adler's usual position during the training mission. The plan had been for Captain Adler to switch positions with the other navigator later in the flight so he could have a turn training in his normal role as navigator during the rest of the mission below the flight deck, while the aircraft continued the low-level terrain-avoidance navigation training exercise.

When the aircraft commander ordered the abandonment of the aircraft, the plane was too low for the crew positions below the flight deck to eject, and subsequently anyone else on that level of the aircraft could not egress either. By this time, they were less than 300 feet AGL and were moving at over 200 knots. The three on the flight deck successfully ejected. The tail gunner was supposed to bail out, but was unable to leave the aircraft.

Of the three that successfully ejected, the pilot's parachute deployed, but he struck a tree and was killed. The aircraft commander, Lieutenant Colonel Dante E. Bulli, came down in a tree 30 feet above the ground. He was able to get down from the tree, but spent the night in weather approaching 28 degrees below zero. Captain Gerald J. Adler ejected from the EWO position and his chute did not open. Captain Adler hit the snow-covered ground in his ejection seat at a force approaching sixteen times the force of gravity (16Gs). He is the only person ever to survive a no-chute ejection sequence at such a force. The wreckage of the vertical stabilizer was found over a mile from the main wreckage on the other side of the mountain.

When I interviewed him, Captain Adler told me that he usually flew in the navigator's position below the flight deck. He had been trained to eject straight down out of the bottom of the aircraft. He said that when ejecting from the lower deck, a mechanism in the seat automatically separates the occupant from the seat after it leaves the aircraft. Adler explained that after the occupant and the seat are automatically separated during the ejection sequence, the chute then deploys automatically.

Captain Adler stated that, as he flew on the flight deck that day, the ejection sequence was slightly different from where he usually flew on the bottom deck. He said that after the seat and occupant eject through the top of the aircraft, there is no automatic mechanism to separate the occupant from the seat and the separation is manual. According to "the book," in the upward ejection seat scenario, the occupant and seat should separate when the seat reaches the top of its arc in its trajectory. Then, the parachute automatically opens. However, the angle that Captain Adler ejected at seemed to have interfered with the expected result.

He recalls remaining in the seat, and his only thought was, "So this is what it's like to eject." There apparently was not enough time to manually separate, and he rode the seat end-over-end to the ground. The seat landed in the snow right side up. If it had not, we would not have these details of this event. If Captain Adler had separated from the seat, he would have been too low for the chute to open, since when he ejected, the aircraft was passing the top of the mountain at about 100 feet above the ground. When the other two on the flight deck ejected, just after passing the top of the mountain, the ground was dropping away from the aircraft and the aircraft commander and pilot's chutes did have time to open.

Captain Adler received a fractured skull, among other injuries, and spent the frigid night in the Maine woods near his ejection seat. He was knocked unconscious when he landed, but when he woke up, it was still light out. Captain Adler got up and saw the smoke from the crash. He said he was only about 200 yards from the main crash site. He could see a lake in the distance and thought it was Moosehead Lake, only learning later that it wasn't.

He attempted to walk down the mountain, but could not do so because the depth of the snow reached his shoulders. Captain Adler returned to his seat and banked snow around it for the night. He could not access his survival kit as it was jammed in the seat, which had bent on impact. Captain Adler wrapped himself up in his parachute. He then lost consciousness again. He woke sometime in the night and saw some aircraft. He attempted to signal them with his flashlight, but learned later that they never saw him.

The temperature neared a dangerous 28 below that night, and he had to survive, cold and wounded, for close to twenty hours before rescue teams found him. Everyone else on board went down with the plane and were found among the pieces of wreckage.

The debris field and two survivors were located the next morning by Maine Warden Service pilots, and military helicopters then responded and rescued the two that morning. By this time, air force personnel were joined by elements of the Maine State Police and the Maine Warden Service. Scott Paper Company Woodland employees began the task of clearing a road through the woods to the crash site. In some places, fifteen feet of drifted snow blocked the way. After the two survivors were located, it was soon realized that the rest of the operation would be a recovery effort.

The Scott Paper Company woodsmen got the ground personnel within a mile of the wreckage. The Maine woods were deep with snow, and it was difficult to find everything that they had come for. The most important task was to recover our missing servicemen from the wreckage. The rescue/recovery teams did what they could.

The classified material was in an aluminum box, which, according to Lindie, was painted international orange with reflective paint on it as well. It was about the size of two manual typewriter cases put together. The box was to be opened by two people with two different keys under the "two-man rule." Nuclear weapons/systems require no less than two people, both being well versed in the task(s) to be performed, in control of them.

Even though Tail Number 53-0406 was not carrying nukes at the time of the accident, it was apparently carrying sensitive information. At that time, a third of all SAC's nuclear forces were armed and either flying or on ground alert at various bases ready to take off in fifteen minutes. During practice alerts and readiness drills, crews manned their aircraft and took off with live nuclear weapons. Still others stood down while undergoing maintenance. Locating any sensitive data was always a high priority, and at this point in the rescue/recovery mission, it had not been found.

Lindie recalled how wonderful the people of Greenville were, and how the town came together during the tragedy. He said they opened a motel that had been closed for the season, as well as local restaurants for the teams. SSgt. Lindie was in Greenville for two more nights before it was decided that further recovery efforts were fruitless. After the accident investigation team completed their work, the air force abandoned the site for the winter. It was assumed by the public that the authorities had gotten everything they had come for, but they hadn't. The wardens and the Maine State Police kept an eye on the area and, for the most part, people stayed away.

After the snow melted, SSgt. Lindie returned as part of a small team of NCOs and a young flight surgeon, put together by the Dow AFB commander, Colonel Grover Y. Greene. Colonel Greene had been a fighter pilot during the Second World War, flying the P-47 Thunderbolt fighter.

The team went to work in the now nearly snow-free area looking for any classified material and any now uncovered remains. What they found in the way of remains were carefully, respectfully, and with dignity placed in plastic containers. The young flight surgeon became physically ill with the discoveries.

They divided the area up into a grid and continued to search for the orange box. Later, when Lindie and the team were taking a smoking break, the base commander approached him. "Sergeant Lindie, good work. I see you've found it," said Colonel Greene. SSgt. Lindie turned around and about twelve feet away, under a log, was the kit. SSgt. Lindie and the men with him were surprised and embarrassed that they had been standing just a few feet from the object of their search. It was, in fact, Colonel Greene who had found the long-sought-for kit. After the recovery of the rest of the remains and the classified material, the wreckage was splashed with yellow paint to indicate to other aircraft that this was a documented crash site and not to be confused in the event of another aircraft accident.

The United States was not in a shooting war with the Russians, but the times were just as urgent due to the stresses between the two nations and their allies. Men and women in our military put it on the line around the clock to keep America safe, and sometimes at the cost of their lives. Seven of nine crewmembers were killed on Elephant Mountain in Maine protecting our freedom, and they should not be forgotten.

The two survivors were Lieutenant Colonel Dante E. Bulli and Captain Gerald J. Adler. The seven souls lost were Lieutenant Colonel Joe R. Simpson, Jr., Major William W. Gabriel, Major Robert J. Morrison, Major Robert J. Hill, Major Herbert L. Hansen, Captain Charles G. Leuchter, and Technical Sergeant Michael F. O'Keefe. Six women were now widowed and nine children had lost their fathers.

Colonel Bulli suffered a crushed ankle and a punctured hand in the incident. In an interview on March 25, 2011, Colonel Bulli told me that it took him about twenty minutes to climb down from the tree before he waited the rest of the night for rescue. The colonel was able to access his survival equipment and he climbed into his sleeping bag for the night. After recovery in the hospital, he would continue with his career in the air force.

Captain Adler had used his parachute for insulation against the cold, as he could not access the MD-1 Survival Kit, containing a sleeping bag, still stuck in his ejection seat. As the captain had lost consciousness at times due to his injuries, he was not able to protect himself any further from the cold and suffered severe frostbite. He told me he received a traumatic brain injury, fractured ribs, frostbitten feet, and double pneumonia, as well as a spinal compression injury. The captain also lost a leg to gangrene. Captain Adler retired from the air force and went on to practice law.

Much of the debris field still remains on Elephant Mountain. The tail gunner's position is now in the center of the area, and several years after the crash a large piece of Monson slate, quarried from the town of Monson about 20 miles south of the site, was erected and stands near it. On the slate are the names of the men of Tail Number 53-0406. Many pay their respects there today, but sadly, others do not understand the magnitude of this silent reminder in the woods, as graffiti and other evidence of disrespect can be found nearby. But what makes our servicemen and women all that much greater is that they know that, and they do the job anyway.

The loss of Tail Number 53-0406 resulted in saving the lives of future crewmembers flying the "BUFF." The understanding of the structural failures of the aircraft led to quick corrections in the fleet of B-52s flying, and those yet to be built.

SSgt. Lindie continued in his career in the air force, retiring as a master sergeant. On October 19, 1963, the sergeant was part of the air force security detail for President John F. Kennedy's arrival at Dow AFB, when the young president appeared at the University of Maine at Orono to receive an honorary degree. SSgt. Lindie's call sign for the detail was "Hyannis Seven." A month later, in November of 1963, there was another very special need for a piece of Monson slate. John F. Kennedy was assassinated in Dallas and it would be Monson slate from the state of Maine that was eventually placed above his head at Arlington National Cemetery.

Retired Master Sergeant William Lindie wanted me to know something else when I interviewed him about the B-52 mishap. He said that later in the summer of 1963, a Mr. Gerald Gartley of Greenville, who owned a gas station and sporting camps there, had gone up to the crash site to take a look around. He found the wallet of one of the crewmen at the wreckage site. Inside, he found a large sum of cash and the identification papers of the serviceman to whom it belonged. Mr. Gartley had come right down off the mountain and driven to the main gate of Dow AFB in Bangor. He soon found himself in the office of the base commander and received the thanks of the air force.

Gerald Gartley was the father of Markham L. Gartley of Greenville. Five years after Gerald Gartley returned the found wallet to the base commander at Dow AFB, Lt. JG Markham (Mark) L. Gartley, USN, flew with the VF-142, the Ghostriders, from an aircraft carrier during the Vietnam War. Lt. JG Gartley was shot down with his Radar Intercept Officer (RIO) flying a Navy F4B Phantom over North Vietnam on August 17, 1968.Mark Gartley was a prisoner of war (POW) in North Vietnam until he was released in 1972 with two other prisoners as a result of a peace movement initiative. His release came a few months before the rest of the American POWs of the Vietnam War were released.

While Mark and other prisoners, including another young American naval aviator by the name of John McCain, were prisoners at the infamous Hanoi Hilton, the students at Colby and other Maine colleges demonstrated against the very real tragedy at Kent State. They eventually also protested against our involvement in Vietnam with other college students around the country. Unfortunately, some of the college demonstrations included the protesting of our men and women in uniform as well.

The Colby march on May 5, 1970, sparked other protest activities. Later in the week, the Air Force Reserve Officer Training Corps (AFROTC) office on campus was occupied for two days by student demonstrators in a "sit-in." The Colby AFROTC professor, United States Air Force Lt. Colonel Don Harris, told me in an interview in 2011 that the students were mainly respectful during the sit-in, and were, for the most part, "just having fun." He remembers one student, however, who was hostile. A few days after the sit-in ended, and at some time during the night, a Molotov cocktail was thrown through the glass of the colonel's office window. When he came to work the following morning, he discovered the device, which had failed to explode because the wick had fallen off while crashing through the window. Colonel Harris had been assigned to Colby as the AFROTC professor after serving honorably in Vietnam, where he flew the B-57 Canberra jet bomber. He remembers being spit upon "at least a half-dozen times" by some students at Colby.

Regardless of your position on the Vietnam War, we should never forget the many that served their country there. A draft was in effect at the time, and those who were drafted did their duty without running away, and made a choice to serve. Some had run off instead to Canada to avoid being drafted. But there were many military roles comprised solely of volunteers—for example, all air force, navy, and marine pilots were volunteers.

A very real tragedy of the Vietnam War was that our returning veterans were many times denied the honor that they deserved. It's one thing to protest the political policy of a nation. It's quite another thing to trample on the honor of the person willing to die to defend it and our way of life. The 58,655 Americans who died in Vietnam did so because they did not run away. Many of those who survived did not wear their uniforms when they returned home for fear of being harassed. We should all strive together to be worthy of their sacrifice.

Mark L. Gartley, the son of the gas station owner who promptly returned the cash-filled wallet of a downed aircraft crewman, continued to serve his country and the people of the State of Maine. The former POW went on to become our secretary of state, and also mounted an unsuccessful run for the United States Senate. Unlike the oft-depicted stereotype of a bitter and broken Vietnam veteran, Gartley has upheld the tradition of service for the sake of service, despite the sacrifice that service extracts.

Chapter 8

SEPTEMBER 13, 2001, BUCKINGHAM PALACE, 1130 HRS.

Comfort Inn, 90 Maine Mall Road, South Portland, Maine, September 10, 2001. Mohamed Atta and Abdul Aziz Al-Omari check in at the motel late that day.

Atta and Al-Omari were observed at Pizza Hut at 415 Main Mall Road. They were photographed at a Key Bank drive-up location at 445 Gorham Road. Next, they were observed in the parking lot of Uno's Restaurant at 280 Maine Mall Road, where a Fast Green ATM photographed the two men. They were later at the Jetport Gas Station located at 446 Western Avenue, South Portland. Lastly, Atta was seen at Walmart, 451 Payne Road in Scarborough, for about twenty minutes. It is believed that is where they purchased box cutters for their mission the next day.

The next morning they checked out of the Comfort Inn and headed for the Portland International Jetport. The men left their 2001 blue Nissan Altima rental car in the parking lot before checking in at the US Airways counter. The men boarded a Colgan Air commuter flight en route to Boston.

In Boston, both Atta and Al-Omari connected to American Airlines Flight 11, a Boeing 767, at Logan International Airport. Mohamed Atta flew the 767-223ER into the North Tower of the World Trade Center in New York City at 0846 Hrs. on 9/11. This crash was followed by United Airlines Flight 175, also originating at Logan International Airport, and also another Boeing, a 767-222. Another group of terrorists flew Flight 175 into the South Tower of the World Trade Center at 0903 Hrs. At

0937, others flew American Airlines Flight 77, a Boeing 757-223, into the Pentagon. At 1003, United Airlines Flight 93, a Boeing 757-222, crashed into a field near Shanksville, Pennsylvania. It is believed that the crash of Flight 93 was due to the efforts of the crew members and passengers who refused to permit their aircraft to be used as yet another terrorist weapon. America was stunned.

The day before, on September 10th, I had started a forty-hour class at the Maine Criminal Justice Academy (MCJA) in Vassalboro. Already a certified MCJA firearms instructor, the class I took prepared me and the other participants to instruct other officers in the deployment and use of the urban assault rifle. Violence in society had finally reached the point where the assault rifle was seen as a viable tool for patrol officers, in addition to the shotgun. There were ten other instructors from all around the state taking the course with me. That first day, a Monday, was spent at the Academy getting familiar with the various weapons systems, as well as breaking down and properly maintaining our own specific weapons. My department utilized the carbine version of the AR-15, but there were a variety of rifles in the class. At the end of the day, we packed up our gear and took it home with instructions to meet the next day at the Capital City Rifle and Pistol Club range in Augusta at 0900 Hrs. The reason for the relatively late start on September 11th was because the rules of Capital City prohibited shooting firearms before 0900, out of respect for the neighborhood residents.

I left my home in Winslow shortly after 0800 Hrs. It was a beautiful, clear morning with a hint of fall in the air. I remember thinking about our second child, Megan, who had started attending Nyack College, a Christian college in Nyack, NY, a few weeks earlier. Meg's boyfriend, Brian Wedge, was there as well. We kind of liked Brian, and Deb and I wondered if they would become serious. Brian was putting himself through college with the help of the army, as he was in the Army Reserve.

I arrived at the range about 0855. The other guys, who had arrived before me, were gathered around a cruiser. One of the guys told me they just heard that a Cessna had accidentally flown into one of the World Trade Center towers in New York. I thought this strange, as the weather forecast I had watched before leaving home had indicated that New York City was clear. Shortly after 0900, it was announced that a 747 had crashed into the other tower. I exclaimed to the guys that this must be "a terrorist attack."

One of our two course instructors was on his cell phone at that time with his sister, a doctor, as I remember, who lived in New York and could see the Twin Towers from her home. He had called her just after the first plane hit, and she told him that she had seen the news report before seeing the smoke from the first tower. The instructor told us that his sister was now hysterical, as she had gone out to look a second time and saw the second aircraft hit.

We hovered around the radios in the various cruisers while the decision was made to continue training this day. It was decided that we would train unless told otherwise by the Academy. We began on the firing range. We would fire one series, and then rush back to a radio in a cruiser to listen for more information. It was soon announced that both airplanes had been airliners, and that this indeed appeared to be a terrorist attack.

One of my fellow students, Maine State Police Trooper Timothy Black, came over to me and asked a bit suspiciously, "Alden, how did you know this was a terrorist attack?"

I replied, "I read Tom Clancy," and explained that this was almost straight out of one of his books.

Trooper Black's pager went off. He was ordered to mobilize and respond to Augusta to assist in the protection of the state government buildings there. The rest of us continued with our training. Just before lunchtime, Maine Criminal Justice Academy Training Coordinator Peter Hall arrived and explained that all state buildings, including the Academy, had been ordered evacuated and closed because of the concern about the possibility of other attacks. We now knew about the attack on the Pentagon and the other airliner that had crashed in Pennsylvania, as well as rumors of attacks on the West Coast. By this time, both the South and the North Towers of the World Trade Center had collapsed, and the casualties were feared to be at least 10,000.

The projected casualties were based on the working population of the buildings. The fact that the number of casualties was actually much lower is directly related to the response of the FDNY and NYPD and other responders. Still, this was the worst sneak attack on the United States in our history, and the first sneak attack on the forty-eight continental states by a foreign enemy against our civilians.

Because we were training outdoors, it was decided that we would continue unless ordered to respond to our various departments. All flights in the U.S. had been grounded, and there was a strange silence we all sensed in the sky due to the lack of the usual air traffic.

If I could not be in place to protect and rescue others or destroy an enemy at this time in our history, I was at the next best place. I was training to do battle, and I was doing so with other warriors.

At the end of the day, we all went home to our families and our TVs. Our oldest son, Shawn, had just graduated from Lancaster Bible College with a degree in pastoral ministries, as he had considered becoming a minister. Shawn was questioning his call to the ministry lately, and wondered if he was called instead to become a police officer. (Later that fall, in fact, Shawn joined the Waterville Police Department as a patrol officer.)

Shawn, my wife, Debora, and Erica, our youngest, watched the coverage with fears that the casualties at the World Trade Center alone would reach 10,000 as predicted by the news media. It wasn't until late that evening that we were able to make contact with our daughter Megan, who was just 20 miles north of New York City, on the Hudson at Nyack. Meg told us that she and Brian could see the smoke from the attacks from their college campus. A few weeks later, Brian and his unit were mobilized.

The officers taking part in the MCJA Urban Rifle Instructors Course continued training through the week. Trooper Black returned to the range the next day, as it had been decided that the state office buildings of Maine were not a target at this time.

On the evening of September 12, 2001, after training at the range, I went to the old house on Winter Street to check on my mother, Myrtle W. Weigelt and her sister Marion B. Jackins. Something drew me there after the attacks. I backed my pickup truck into the driveway and Aunt Marion met me outside by the vehicle. She had tears in her eyes and she threw her arms around my neck. While still hugging me, she exclaimed in a tearful whisper, "Now you know how we felt after Pearl Harbor."

And for the first time, I connected with her generation and all the stories that I had grown up with. There was no denying that I now knew how they had felt. I went in to see my mother. She was watching the continuing coverage on Fox News, and she was mad as hell. And somehow it felt good to share this emotion with her as one of the "Greatest Generation." I brought my AR in and laid it on the dining room table. I broke it down and cleaned it right there at Winter Street as Mom, Aunt Marion, and I continued to watch the coverage.

After training on the range the next day, I checked on Mom and Aunt Marion. Mom mentioned that our national anthem had been played at Buckingham Palace that day. I didn't know why at the time, but this gesture by the British seemed to soothe me. I took my responsibility as a police officer and my oath to serve and uphold the Constitution of the United States very seriously, and until this time, I had felt as if the United States stood alone in the aftermath of the attacks. I soon learned that there had been demonstrations in Israel in support of the United States. In many Arab nations, however, there had been celebrations in support of the attacks.

I later learned the details about the playing of the anthem at

Buckingham Palace. On September 13, 2001, at about 1115 Hrs., the Band of the Coldstream Guards marched out of Wellington Barracks on Bird Cage Walk near St. James Park, marching the short distance toward Buckingham Palace as they do during every changing of the guard ceremony. The Coldstream Guards are the oldest surviving regiment in the British Army, dating back to 1650.

In attendance for the ceremony were HRH Prince Andrew, Duke of York, and the U.S. ambassador, Mr. William Farish. The American tourists around Buckingham Palace were there as usual that day, as well as others from all over the world. Many of them were unable to return home because planes were still grounded in the United States following the horror of the previous days.

I mentioned in Chapter 2 that in 1814 the United States and Great Britain had written some beautiful music together. And the music had been written with the blood of the warriors of both our nations at the time. The words of the "Star-Spangled Banner" were by American Francis Scott Key and the music was by the English Composer John Stafford Smith. But we were yet to play that music together...here...like this. Oh sure, the British had played our national anthem during state visits, as we had played theirs during state visits to the United States. But the national anthem of the United States had never been played during the changing of the guard ceremony at the home of the Sovereign of Great Britain on an occasion such as this. And, if you remember, every time we sing our "My Country, 'Tis of Thee," we are singing words set to the music of the British national anthem, which is now called "God Save the Queen."

At the proper time in the ceremony on September 13, 2001, and for the first time in the history of our two nations, and by the order of "Elizabeth the Second, by the Grace of God, of the United Kingdom of Great Britain and Northern Ireland and of Her other Realms and Territories Queen, Head of the Commonwealth, Defender of the Faith,"...and, not to mention, in Her Majesty's own front yard, the "Star-Spangled Banner" was played at Buckingham Palace. After a two-minute moment of silence, the band played other "sombre American music, including 'Hymn to the Fallen' by the composer John Williams and used during the closing credits in *Saving Private Ryan.*"

When the Coldstream Guards struck up the American national anthem, most of the Americans in the crowd put their right hands over their hearts, and many sang the words while the band of the Coldstream Guards played. At the end of the anthem, there was applause and, for many, tears. Her Majesty would return later that week from holiday to meet with Ambassador Farish and his wife. She offered the condolences, friendship, and solidarity of the British people to the people of the United States. And hopefully, many will remember this gesture of friendship and respect for the rest of their lives.

On September 14, 2001, there was a memorial service at St. Paul's Cathedral in London. Her Majesty The Queen and Prime Minister Tony Blair attended, along with U.S. Ambassador William Farish. The cathedral was at capacity, and speakers had been set up outside so those amassed there could listen and participate. The "Star-Spangled Banner" was played and sung there as well. It was later said that Her Majesty sung all the words to our anthem with the rest of those mourning those lost of just a few days before.

Later in the service the American "Battle Hymn of the Republic" was sung by the congregation, but this was not the first time this hymn was played here.

It was here at St. Paul's that in 1958 Her Majesty The Queen, this very same Elizabeth, had dedicated the American Chapel in one of the most revered locations inside the cathedral. The chapel is located behind the high altar, and was dedicated to the more than 28,000 American military personnel who were stationed in England and gave their lives for liberty during the Second World War. Remember Chapter 1, *Sentimental Journey*, and the Jimmy Stewart of Chapter 4, who flew for the Eighth Air Force? The Eighth Air Force was based in England and flew against Germany from there. The Eighth Air Force lost more than 26,000 of the more than 28,000 souls remembered at the American Chapel in this house of worship that is St. Paul's.

It was then that I started truly believing that America was not alone. On that same day, September 14, 2001, DDG 81, an Arleigh Burke–class destroyer built at Bath Iron Works in Maine, received honors from the Dutch Marine destroyer *Lutjens* as she passed abeam. The crew of the *Lutjens* hoisted the Stars and Stripes to half-staff and manned her rails in support of the United States.

In addition to the Stars and Stripes, flying from the mast of the American destroyer DDG 81 is the British Royal Navy's White Ensign, which always flies from this same mast. That is because DDG 81's christened name is the USS *Winston S. Churchill*. In honor of her namesake, there is at all times a Royal Navy officer assigned to her crew. It was Churchill's daughter, Lady Mary Soames, who participated in her christening during her launch at Bath Iron Works.

To be true to Mr. Churchill's memory, we should also remember something else about him. Churchill had made his wishes known for his own funeral when the time came. After the officers of the Grenadier

Guards carried his casket into Saint Paul's Cathedral in January of 1965, the hymn sung at his request was the American "Battle Hymn of the Republic."

The hymn was also played here, two years before Mr. Churchill's funeral, when it was played in honor of a young American president, who was remembered by the British, after his assassination in November of 1963.

That same president, John F. Kennedy, had previously declared by proclamation, as authorized by Congress, Winston Churchill an Honorary Citizen of the United States earlier in April of 1963. Mr. Churchill was not well enough to travel to the United States at the time and his son accepted the honor on behalf of his father from President Kennedy.

Not only had Mr. Churchill's mother been born an American, he was also a scholar of, and had written extensively on, the American Civil War. It is my opinion that Mr. Churchill also loved America.

At the time of 9/11, I did not fully understand the bond between the United States and the British people, but I was beginning to, and I would strive to learn more.

Chapter 9

IN HIS MAJESTY'S SERVICE, SEBAGO LAKE, MAINE

Retired Master Sergeant William Lindie told me of an experience he had as a ten-year-old boy living in Searsport, Maine, in 1944. He had been down by the bay where the Liberty Ships docked to load up on munitions before heading across the Atlantic to England. The beach was full of pebbles that the young Lindie skipped out onto the water, the background noise of the soft ocean waves rolling onto this protected beach no doubt adding to nautical daydreams. Suddenly, two aircraft speeding toward shore right down on the deck startled him. They came so fast that he fell over backward trying to keep them in sight. Lying on his back, he watched them go by, and saw the bull's-eye emblem of the British under their wings. Lindie said that both aircraft had been fighters, but it would not be until 2010 that his memory was confirmed and his puzzlement over why the British were in America in 1944 was answered.

The Second World War started a little more than two years prior to the Japanese attack on Pearl Harbor on December 7, 1941. It began with the Nazi invasion of Poland in September of 1939. This resulted in a declaration of war by France and the British Empire against Germany. France would fall in the spring of 1940, and then the British Empire and her Commonwealth would stand... alone. And at the same time, England prepared for invasion by the Nazis.

Prime Minister Winston Churchill led and encouraged the British people with his determination and guts. In an interview about her memories of Mr. Churchill, his former daughter-in-law, Pamela Harriman, recalled a conversation at the dinner table one evening. She recalled that Churchill was brooding over dinner. He had recently remarked in a speech to the House of Commons on June 4, 1940, "We shall fight on the beaches, we shall fight on the landing grounds, we shall fight in the fields and in the streets, we shall fight in the hills; we shall never surrender, and even if, which I do not for a moment believe, this Island or a large part of it were subjugated and starving, then our Empire beyond the seas, armed and guarded by the British Fleet, would carry on the struggle, until, in God's good time, the New World, with all its power and might, steps forth to the rescue and liberation of the old."

Mr. Churchill said to no one in particular at the dinner table that evening, as if he were talking to himself, "You can each take a dead German with you." Pamela responded that she did not have a gun, nor did she know how to shoot one. To which Mr. Churchill replied, "You can go into the kitchen and get a carving knife!"

On June 18, 1940, Churchill spoke to the Commons again, proclaiming, "But if we fail, then the whole world, including the United States, including all that we have known and cared for, will sink into the abyss of a new dark age made more sinister, and perhaps more protracted, by the lights of perverted science. Let us therefore brace ourselves to our duties, and so bear ourselves, that if the British Empire and its Commonwealth last for a thousand years, men will still say, 'This was their finest hour.'"

In the United States, President Roosevelt did not have the support of the American people in getting involved in this war. America had been involved with Britain and her allies during the Great War just two decades earlier, and there was a great deal of antiwar sentiment at the time. However, Roosevelt knew that it was just a matter of time before we were involved. And many believed he wanted to come to the aid of the British people and stop Hitler, but he could not do so militarily...yet.

Then the Germans began to soften up England in preparation for invasion. During the summer of 1940, they began the systematic destruction of the Royal Air Force (RAF) in what would be known as the Battle of Britain. They bombed the airfields of the RAF and aircraft production factories in an attempt to achieve air superiority prior to an invasion. Eventually, the bombing shifted to London after a retaliatory strike against Berlin by the British. The bombing of London was later referred to by her citizens as "the Blitz."

This proved a fatal error on the part of the Germans because the shift in target to London from the resources of the RAF allowed the RAF to continue to be a viable threat to the German bombers. The Germans lost the initiative and the invasion never happened, but they continued to bomb the British. During the Blitz, between September 7, 1940, and May 16, 1941, war casualties in England, mostly in and around London, were approximately 43,000 civilians.

Prime Minister Winston Churchill, King George VI, and his queen, Elizabeth, refused to leave London during the Blitz. The Prime Minister often went out into the streets to tour the bomb damage in the city. The King and Queen would do so as well. Churchill's visibility, and that of the King and Queen, rallied the people. When Buckingham Palace was bombed, this furthered the bond between the British people and the Royal Family. The people knew their leaders were in touch with them, shared their fate, and, as the world would soon learn and the title of a short documentary film of the time proclaimed, *London Can Take It!*

During the bombing, Churchill sometimes went up to the rooftop of one of the government buildings in Whitehall to watch. In an interview, one of Churchill's former secretaries, Marian Holmes, recalled one such occasion. She said that the bombing was pretty heavy that day and was occurring in the vicinity of St. James Park, which is also close to Buckingham Palace and Whitehall. Marian Holmes said that Winston Churchill asked her, "Are you frightened, Miss Holmes? Are you sure you're not frightened?" and she replied "No, I'm not frightened." Marian Holmes told the interviewer that "it was impossible to be frightened in his presence."

Later in the war, between June 1944 and March 1945, the Nazis use of the "Vengeance Weapons" began. The V1 Flying Bomb was a primitive cruise-missile type of weapon, and fighters eventually learned how to intercept them. The V2, however, was a ballistic-missile type of weapon, and against these there was no defense or warning. The V2 approached its target at supersonic speeds, and the only warning was the destruction of the target. Another 8,938 civilians lost their lives to these.

On August 20, 1940, at the height of the Battle of Britain, Winston Churchill spoke again to the House of Commons. He addressed the Commons, the nation, and ultimately, the world in regard to the ongoing efforts of the RAF. "Never in the field of human conflict was so much owed by so many to so few." And here it is. Included in the "so many" that owed so much "to so few" was the United States and the rest of the world.

I've already said this, but it deserves repeating: Great Britain and her Commonwealth stood alone! It was two years before the "New World" came to the aid of the old. And if Great Britain hadn't been able to stand, the world would be a very different place today, and no doubt would have sunk into the "abyss." The New World, too, would be attacked on December 7, 1941, and would stand with the old—and together we would stand against, and eventually destroy, one of the most vile, evil regimes in the history of mankind.

In January of 2010, Debora and I were once again at Barnes & Noble, our favorite bookstore in Augusta. I was in the history section as usual when Deb came back to me with a magazine she had located and told me to take a look at the cover. The magazine was the December 2009 issue of *Britain at War Magazine*. The cover article was "Corsairs in the Lake." I looked at the article and learned that two American-made Chance Vought F4U Corsair fighters that had collided and crashed on May 16, 1944, had been recently discovered at the bottom of Sebago Lake in Maine.

I also read that they had been flown by two British Royal Navy pilots who had been lost with the planes and were still at the bottom of the lake. To say the least, I was both puzzled and very curious, and would strive to learn more. I learned much from the article and continued my search. The website www.hms-vengeance.co.uk is the website of the British World War Two aircraft carrier HMS *Vengeance*. This is a good resource for information about this topic, as is the website for the Fleet Air Arm Archive, http://fleetairarmarchive.net.

During World War II, under the Lend-Lease program, fifty percent of all British Royal Navy pilots were trained in the United States. Lend-Lease was the program under which the United States supplied the United Kingdom, the Soviet Union, China, France, and other Allied nations with war materials; it was signed into law in March of 1941. Under Lend-Lease, the U.S. shipped materials to the Allies in return for services, supplies, and military facilities overseas. The materials sent by the United States were to be used until such time as their return or destruction.

President Roosevelt had coined a phrase and referred to the United States as the "Arsenal of Democracy" while proposing the concept earlier in December of 1940. Roosevelt believed in the plight of the British, but could do no more at the time due to the political power of U.S. isolationists and organizations such as America First.

A few months prior, in September of 1940, the first gesture of help toward the British was a program known as Destroyers for Bases. At the request of Winston Churchill, the United States had loaned the Royal Navy 50 mothballed destroyers in return for 99-year leases of British Empire property in the West Indies to be used as U.S. military bases.

In the United States, the Fleet Air Arm of the Royal Navy accounting base was in Washington, D.C., and was commissioned in the Royal Navy as HMS *Saker*. The U.S. Navy base at Lewiston, Maine, was commissioned under HMS *Saker* in 1943, and acted as the parent ship for all Fleet Air Arm facilities in the U.S.A. Royal Navy land bases and headquarters were commissioned as ships were in the Royal Navy, hence the HMS (His Majesty's Ship) moniker before the name. This also served as a way to confuse the enemy with regard to communication traffic they intercepted. In this way, there were more commissioned ships believed to exist than actually did.

When the Royal Navy training squadrons arrived in Lewiston, Maine, they had already received their basic flight training. It was in Maine that the pilots received further training and were fine-tuned in the British style of formation flying in the actual combat aircraft they would fly in war. The fighter aircraft included the Wildcat and Corsair, and of these, the Chance Vought F4U Corsair was the newest and hottest fighter of the day. These squadrons were training up to operational status. When found ready, they deployed to carrier qualification training farther down the East Coast. The version of the Corsair that the British flew had its wings modified and shortened by eight inches due to the lower ceilings on the hangar decks of British aircraft carriers.

The Corsair had the distinctive gull-wing design. It also had a very long engine cowling to house its 18-cylinder, 2000-horsepower, radial engine. This made the Corsair difficult to land on an aircraft carrier because on a straight-in final approach the pilot could not see over the nose or, more importantly, see the landing signal officer (LSO) either. The U.S. Navy did not like it for this reason, and was reluctant to make it operational from aircraft carriers. For the time being, the Corsair was operated from forward land-based strips by the U.S. Marines.

It was the Royal Navy that eventually figured out and perfected a new style of continuous-turn approach to landing that in time caught on with the U.S. Navy. Ultimately, the Corsair became a very operationally effective carrier fighter with the U.S. Navy, as well as with the British.

From 1943 to 1945, it was in Maine that many of the British pilots learned to fly the F4U Corsair in the British traditional attack formation. It was also in Maine that the Royal Navy lost about 177 Corsairs in training accidents, according to *Britain at War Magazine*. The names of the British flying officers lost in Sebago Lake on May 16, 1944, who are still considered missing 67 years later by the British Ministry of Defense, are Sub-Lieutenant Raymond Laurence Knott and Sub-Lieutenant Vaughan Reginald Gill. The Historic Aircraft Recovery Corporation (HARC) had located the wreck site in Sebago Lake of one of the aircraft and began legal preparations to salvage it.

The interesting points of the matter are that these aircraft were

American-made and were being used by the British under Lend-Lease. According to Lend-Lease, the aircraft were to be accounted for and returned after hostilities ended, but these two aircraft were obviously lost.

Another fact is that the wrecks are also the graves of British military personnel whose bodies were never recovered. Parties of interest in the matter, in addition to the HARC, are the governments of the United States and the United Kingdom. Court decisions eventually dictated that it was ultimately up to the British Ministry of Defense (MOD) to determine what happened to their lost pilots. At the time of this writing, the decision had been reached by the MOD that Sebago Lake would be the final resting place of their lost pilots, and therefore HARC could not disturb the wrecks.

I wonder how many people who come to the Sebago region for their vacation time know of the sacrifice that took place there 67 years ago.

Chapter 10

U.S. NAVAL CEMETERY, PORTSMOUTH NAVAL SHIPYARD, KITTERY, MAINE

Norman McKinstry's family lived in the British West Indies. Norman had been sent to school at Dover College in England by his parents. Norman's two sisters were sent to school in Kent, England. It was the custom of British families of means living in the British Colonies to send their children back to England for their education. The only problem was that this was June of 1940, the start of the Battle of Britain, and the McKinstry children had a front-row seat.

The Battle of Britain largely took place over and around Kent and Dover as the German bombers were intercepted by the RAF on their way to their intended targets, which included the city of London. To reach London from France, where many of the German bombers were based, one must fly across the English Channel. Often, they flew over Dover or Kent on their way.

The McKinstrys and other children and families were sent home. The convoy that the McKinstry children found themselves on formed up at Milford Haven, Wales. While they waited to leave, the Germans dropped mines from aircraft into the ocean during the night, delaying the convoy. Instead of hitting their intended target—the ocean—two of the mines impacted and blew up two of the ships in the convoy.

Luckily, Norman McKinstry and his sisters made it to Jamaica. Norman's father was the British Attorney General of British Honduras, and Norman had grown up there. Norman enrolled in Munroe College, Jamaica, and graduated in June of 1942. Mr. McKinstry explained to me that there was no mandatory service for British citizens living in the colonies. His father wanted him to go to Cambridge University to study law, but Norman had other ideas. He enlisted for "Hostilities Only in the Royal Navy Volunteer Reserves." He could not accept the idea of continuing in school as a "healthy eighteen-year-old" while Britain was at war. In his autobiographical paper titled "A British Cadet's Odyssey to NAS Grosse Ile and Beyond," he wrote, "I just knew that would not work!!!!"

From there, Norman headed back to England for boot camp near Portsmouth. After boot camp, he went to another base where they were trained up to naval airmen. Of the 350 graduates of the course, half trained in Britain and half trained in the United States. Mr. McKinstry said that since he had grown up in the British West Indies, he was already westernized. He listened to American radio and ate cornflakes for breakfast. While in England, he found the food different and strange from what he was used to at home. Mr. McKinstry said that when they asked the 350 graduates of the course how many wanted to continue their training in the United States, his hand immediately flew up.

The 175 British Aviation Cadets were sent to the United States on the *Queen Mary*, which had been converted to a troop ship during the war. They eventually arrived at Grosse Ile, Michigan, for primary aviation training during the summer of 1943. From November of 1943 to April of 1944, Norman and the other cadets continued their training at Pensacola, Florida. It would be there, on April 14, 1944, that Norman McKinstry received his wings. After Pensacola, half the class went to Jacksonville for fighter training and the other half went to Ft. Lauderdale or Vero Beach for torpedo bomber training. Norman went to Jacksonville, as he had been selected to fly fighters. And the training was dangerous. In Jacksonville, while completing basic fighter training, Norman lost two roommates to training accidents.

Though they never met, Norman later learned that while he was at Pensacola there was an American navy pilot trainee there at the same time by the name of George H.W. Bush, who someday would become the president of the United States.

After Jacksonville, Norman McKinstry came to Maine. He was first assigned to Training Squadron 738 after arriving at HMS *Saker*, Lewiston, Maine, in May of 1944. Training Squadron 738 was a second-line training squadron where primary training in the F4U Corsair fighter took place. Norman's class moved up to first-line training, being assigned to the No. 1849 Royal Navy Squadron, where that training brought the pilot closer to operational status.

These squadrons were based in Maine and flew out of Brunswick

Naval Air Station, which had gotten its start as a military base that trained Royal Navy pilots. The instructors were mostly American navy and marine personnel. Sub-Lieutenant Norman McKinstry, Royal Navy Volunteer Reserve (RNVR), trained in Maine in the aircraft that took him to war, the Chance Vought F4U Corsair. It was in Maine that he learned the art of British formation flying and prepared for carrier approaches and landings. The airfield at Trenton, Maine, where I toured and flew in *Sentimental Journey* from, was set up as a carrier deck so that mock carrier landings and approaches could be practiced by the British pilots. They flew all around the state as well.

And there were a number of accidents in Maine, too. The story in *Britain at War Magazine* stated that no less than 177 Corsairs were lost in training accidents in Maine alone. I asked Mr. McKinstry about this statistic, and he thought it about right. Although not all the airmen in the accidents were killed, many were.

It was here that Norman lost his third roommate, Sub-Lieutenant Peter John Haxell Cann on July 21, 1944, when he crashed on Cottle Hill in Mount Vernon, Maine. From then on, no one wanted to bunk with Norman, and he would have a room to himself. Two other classmates of Norman's were lost also. Sub-Lieutenant Howard R. Bouchard and Sub-Lieutenant Christopher P. Grunhill were killed in a midair collision with each other on September 11, 1944, near Brunswick Naval Air Station.

The flying in Maine was dangerous as these young men got up to speed with the newest and hottest fighter aircraft of the day, but it was thrilling and fun as well. The British fighter doctrine was to attack in formation, so there was a lot of formation tactics training and a lot of accidents, too. The pilots were also expected to attack on the deck at treetop level.

Mr. McKinstry recalled coming back to base after a low-level treetop practice run, and it was soon discovered that one of his fellow pilots had some Maine pine needles and the remains of some pine cones in the oil cooler air intakes at the root of his wings. There was also a crack discovered in one of his main wing spars. The pilot never felt the impact, and it could have been a lot worse. Things happen kind of fast when you're low and at 300 knots.

One fine afternoon in June 1944, Norman was in the area of Lake Winnipesaukee in New Hampshire. He approached the lake from the direction of Meredith and dropped down on the deck over the water. He spotted an 18-foot day-sailer with a man and woman on board. Norman was flying at about 300 knots, and he was below the height of their mast. He headed for the sailboat. Just before reaching it, he hauled back on the stick and the F4U immediately climbed. His prop wash knocked the sailboat over on its side, and the couple went into the water. He said he "got the hell out of there" before someone got his numbers.

Sub-Lieutenant Norman McKinstry, RNVR, was a fighter pilot, and he was expected to be aggressive. He said the mature cadets became bomber pilots as they were responsible for the other people in their crews.

It would be in Maine that Norman met a woman named Ruth at a USO dance in Lewiston. She was chaperoning a group of college women at the dance, and he said that when they met, they seemed to hit it off right away.

After training in Maine, the squadron went to Norfolk, Virginia, for carrier qualifications. Then the No. 1849 Royal Navy Squadron was assigned to the aircraft carrier HMS *Vengeance*, where they were combined and merged into Squadron 1850. They now were combat operational.

Norman McKinstry survived the war. He flew the F4U Corsair and also had experience flying the Supermarine Seafire, which was the Royal Navy version of the famous Supermarine Spitfire of Battle of Britain fame. Mr. McKinstry told me that the Seafire was a beautiful airplane to fly and handled like a dream, but he said that if he were going to war, he would rather be in a Corsair due to the armor that protected the pilot.

As soon as he could, he returned to the United States, and Ruth met him in New York City. They got engaged and, soon afterwards, were married. After the war, Norman got a job in radio at WLAM, AM 1470 "on your dial" in Lewiston. Norman did a little of everything, including broadcasting, management, and sales. He then went to Sears and started there as a salesman. One day, a young lady by the name of Woolworth came into the store and Norman ended up selling her the biggest freezer that Sears had. After the sale, other employees told him that the lady was the Woolworth of the famous store chain.

From there, Norman went into the management of a furniture manufacturing company in Massachusetts. Norman and Ruth later bought the Sesuit Harbor Motel in East Dennis, on Cape Cod. It would be here that Norman finally retired after raising a family.

When I first made contact with Mr. McKinstry, it was a few days after Ruth, his wife of almost 65 years, had passed away. Norman still builds and flies radio-controlled aircraft, and at age 86, he was still playing tennis twice a week.

During the war years, there was a lot of military and war-effort activity in Maine. Portland was home to the U.S. Navy's North Atlantic Fleet. In South Portland, they built the famous Liberty Ships. Many convoys formed up here, and others passed by on their way to England and North Africa.

Many U.S. Army Air Force planes on their way to Europe stopped and refueled in Maine. The Civil Air Patrol provided submarine patrol, the British Royal Navy trained here, and the U.S. Navy patrolled the coast. Between December 7, 1941, and Victory in Japan Day on August 14, 1945, more than 100 of these pilots and aircrew members lost their lives in our state. Details of these sacrifices can be found on the Aviation Archaeology in Maine website, http://mainewreckchasers.com.

The State of Maine has always had a history with the sea. Mainers have built ships, sailed in them, and also fought and died in them. The Portsmouth Naval Shipyard in Kittery, Maine (Maine recently won a border dispute with New Hampshire over which state the shipyard is in), has been building and servicing warships ever since 1690, when we were still a British colony. On the grounds of the shipyard is a small cemetery. It is the U.S. Naval Cemetery of the Portsmouth Naval Shipyard. There have been 186 buried there since the first burial in 1820, including many from the U.S. Navy and Marines, as well as some military spouses. The cemetery is not open to the public because the shipyard is a military installation.

There are thirteen Royal Navy pilots buried there as well. Eleven of these men were killed in crashes during their training in Maine during the war. Two of these crashes occurred a short distance from my home in Central Maine, in the towns of Clinton and Mount Vernon. Three of these men were squadron-mates of Norman McKinstry, and one of these was his last roommate. One pilot died in a fire at Brunswick Naval Air Station and one pilot died of sickness. There is also a Royal Navy mechanic buried there, as well as an RAF sergeant who was killed by a hit-and-run driver.

When the British steamship S.S. *Empire Knight* wrecked off the Maine coast in February of 1944, five of her British seamen and eleven of her Danish seamen were lost. These young men from Great Britain and Denmark also found rest at the Naval Cemetery, buried on American soil and a long way from home. There were two pilots lost who at the time served in His Majesty's Royal Navy. They are still considered missing from Her Majesty's Royal Navy of today. They came to Maine with the others in 1943 and 1944. Then, here in Maine, they gave "all that man can give, life itself...for the sacred cause of justice and the freedom of the world." Their final resting place is somewhere in the waters of Sebago Lake.

There were also many American military flyers killed in flying accidents in Maine, both during and after the war. My prayer is that none of us ever forget.

Peter J.H. Cann Sub-Lieutenant RNVR. Mr. McKinstry's last roommate. (U.S. Navy photograph. Printed by permission of the U.S. Navy)

Chapter 11

NEW ENGLAND SHIPBUILDING CORP., SOUTH PORTLAND, MAINE, AND ANOTHER MEMBER OF THE "GREATEST GENERATION"

Wolfgang Egon was born in Danzig, Germany on October 7, 1902. He arrived in New York on September 9, 1909, just a month before he turned seven on the steamship S.S. *Pennsylvania*. Wolf was the sixth of eight children. The oldest, Max Ferdinand J., had come to America with his father, Franz Ludwig, the year before to help establish the family import business before sending for the rest of the family.

Six of the children, Ilse, Harry, Gerda, Margot, Wolfgang, and Giesela, traveled on the *Pennsylvania* with their mother, Emma Anna. The youngest, Guenther, was just nine months old when his mother, brothers, and sisters left for America. He had to be left behind, as he had become ill, and on the advice of a physician could not make the journey. He was left with relatives in Germany because the family's passage was paid for and there were no refunds. Guenther remained in Germany until after World War I. His family did not learn until several years later that the money they sent to their relatives for Guenther's care was not ultimately spent on him, and he ran the streets until his family in America could arrange for his passage. Franz Ludwig's American business partner later ran off with the assets of the import business, leaving Franz and his family with the debt.

Franz Ludwig was Prussian and his wife, Emma, was Austrian. Emma's father had been the manager of the Vienna Opera. Emma told her children the story of how she and her parents had stayed, along with the opera company, at the summer palace of the Emperor of Austria, Franz Joseph I. Emma also recalled presenting the emperor with a bouquet of flowers when she was a little girl.

Wolfgang Egon's formal education only went as far as grammar school. When Wolf was about 15 or 16 and in the sixth grade, a young sculptor by the name of Rudulph Evans came to the class in search of a young man to serve as a model for his new work, *Boy and Panther*, based on Rudyard Kipling's Mowgli character from *The Jungle Book*.

The statue was commissioned by the family of American banker and former Assistant Treasurer of the United States, Frank A. Vanderlip. Wolf lived with the sculptor for about a year while Evans worked on the statue. Today, *Boy and Panther* is on display at Brookgreen Gardens in South Carolina, which has a significant collection of American sculpture.

Wolf became a protégé of the sculptor, and with Evans's sponsorship, eventually attended art school to study sculpture at the prestigious Beaux-Arts in New York. Rudulph Evans went on to sculpt the statue of Thomas Jefferson for the world-renowned Jefferson Memorial in Washington, D.C.

A few years before his death in 1983, Wolf was contacted by Tescia Ann Yonkers, a young lady working on her doctoral thesis about Rudulph Evans. The Vanderlip family had placed Tescia in contact with Wolf. Wolf provided Tescia with much firsthand information he had about Evans. Later, Tescia wrote *Shrine of Freedom* for the U.S. Park Service, which discussed the Jefferson Memorial and Evans.

While *Boy and Panther* was being created, Frank Vanderlip invited Wolfgang to come to his home and meet his children. Wolf stayed with the Vanderlips for about a week. Mr. Vanderlip wanted his children exposed to a kid from the lower class. Frank's son, Frank A. Vanderlip, Jr., and Wolf quickly became friends. The friendship continued for the rest of their lives through correspondence. In Wolf's papers is a personal reply, dated July 12, 1937, from Narcissa Vanderlip after Wolf wrote her regarding the death of her husband, Frank A. Vanderlip Sr., the father of his friend.

Wolf lost two of his siblings after coming to America. Ilse died in 1913 from appendicitis. In the winter of 1919, when Wolf was 16, he and his older brother, Harry, went ice skating on a pond. They both fell through the ice. Thankfully, they were not in over their heads, and they managed to climb out. Emma put her two sons to bed, but Wolf snuck out of the house and continued to play. Harry came down with pneumonia and died on February 4, 1919. Wolf was convinced that the reason for his own survival was that he continued to work up a sweat skating, and that warded off any sickness. This determination and personal toughness characterized Wolf for the rest of his life.

Wolf's oldest brother, Max, became a musician and had a magic act on a British ocean liner with an English woman as his assistant. Just before World War I started, a German warship stopped the ocean liner. Max had never obtained his American citizenship, so since he was still considered German, he was taken off the ship by the Germans and forced into the German army and forced to fight on the Russian Front in WW I.

After the war, Max worked as a cook on a German ship. When the ship visited Argentina, Max jumped ship. For many years he ran into the hills every time a German ship was in port. Max changed his name to Harry, after his deceased brother, and eventually formed and conducted his own orchestra in Buenos Aires. His orchestra was a favorite of the Argentine dictator Juan Perón.

At Beaux-Arts, Wolf met his first wife, Doris. They married when Wolf was 18 and Doris was 19. Art did not earn a living for Wolf, and in 1924 he took work at the brokerage house of J. D. Frankel & Co., located at 50 Broad Street in New York City. He started there as a runner, moved up to stock recorder, and then worked in the clearinghouse order department. In 1928, Wolf changed firms to E. B. Smith & Co., 31 Nassau Street in New York City.

On November 24, 1928, Wolfgang's father, Franz Ludwig, gave a speech to the German-American organization he belonged to known as the Schlaraffia. This was an organization for philosophical Germans, and at one time Albert Einstein had reportedly made an address to them. After giving the speech, Franz sat down in his chair and passed away suddenly. Wolf and his brother Guenther later attended a memorial service for their father at a meeting of the Schlaraffia. Wolf stood up and chastised the group for speaking in German during the service as was their custom during their meetings. Wolf said, "You are Americans now," and should "speak English as Americans." Wolf continued to receive the organization's literature for several years. However, he grew increasingly concerned about the tone and content of Schlaraffia's mailings, and sent his concerns to the Federal Bureau of Investigation.

In September of 1929, Wolf and Doris bought a farm, sight unseen, in Freedom, Maine. They planned to move to Maine the following spring and begin working the farm. On Black Thursday, October 24, 1929, while Wolf was still employed at E. B. Smith, the stock market crash occurred. The crash put into motion events leading to the Great Depression. Wolf recalled people he knew who jumped out of windows to their deaths on

Wall Street because of the financial devastation that had overtaken them. Wolf witnessed some of these acts of desperation, but he miraculously kept his job until May of 1930, when he and Doris came to Maine.

Wolf and Doris attempted to make a go of the farm, but they were unsuccessful. They worked at various jobs in Waterville until moving to Seattle, Washington, for about a year to try their luck there. They returned to Waterville, where they eventually divorced but remained friends. They both worked on and off at the photographic studio called the Preble Studio at 68 Main Street in Waterville. Wolf learned the work of the darkroom at the studio, while Doris retouched negatives and learned how to take photo portraits. Wolf also worked at Farrar Brown, an auto parts store on Silver Street in Waterville.

While living in Waterville, Wolf finally became an American citizen on December 2, 1931. Wolf attended Parks Air College in St. Louis from November of 1933 to March of 1934 and studied to be an aircraft mechanic, but it was in Waterville that he met and later married his second wife.

Wolf and his second wife, Myrtle, married on August 17, 1941. A little over three months later, the Japanese bombed Pearl Harbor. Wolf prepared to go into the military. His wife became pregnant with their first son, Robert. When his number came up in the draft, the law had just been changed and he was too old to be drafted. If it hadn't been for the fact that his wife was carrying his first child, he would have joined anyway.

In 1940, at Cushing Point in South Portland, Maine, work commenced on a shipyard to build thirty Ocean Class ships for Britain. The Todd-Bath Iron Shipbuilding Corporation was to the east of Bug Light at Cushing Point. Britain desperately needed cargo ships and, as previously stated, Britain stood alone. Work was soon under way on a second shipyard, the South Portland Shipbuilding Corporation, which was to the west of Cushing Point. With war on the horizon, the United States also needed ships, and by law, the two shipyards had to remain separate as America was still officially neutral.

After Pearl Harbor, however, the yards were combined into the New England Shipbuilding Corporation. Together, the two yards turned out a total of 274 ships, including the thirty Ocean Class ships built for Britain. At the peak of production, 30,000 employees worked in the yards, including approximately 3700 women, and many of whom earned the nickname "Rosie the Riveter." Many of these ships never made it to their destinations, as they became targets of war. Along with the destroyed ships, many souls sank with them.

Wolfgang worked for the South Portland Shipbuilding Corporation

Liberty Ship Memorial South Portland, Maine (Photo by Alden Weigelt)

between July of 1942 and September of 1943. The increasing needs of the shipyard slowly took over the community of Cushing Point to the point that it no longer existed as a community. People's homes and ways of life were sacrificed for the war effort. This was a different type of sacrifice, but a sacrifice just the same. There is now a memorial plaque in place where the community that once stood at Cushing Point had vanished; the shipyards met the same fate after the war was over.

While Wolf worked in the shipyards, an agent of the Federal Bureau of Investigation approached him. The FBI was interested in Wolf for a number of reasons. One had to do with Wolf's German heritage. Another reason may have been due to Wolf's previous report to the FBI regarding his concerns about the Schlaraffia's growing Nazi sympathy. In any event, the FBI thought that he might be of use. As he had a German first and last name, he might be approached to have his politics tested by a Nazi sympathizer. The FBI also thought he might be able to spot German mannerisms, phrases, or characteristics in others.

Wolfgang reported to his FBI contact on a regular basis, and his willingness to cooperate was not without risk. He had a couple of close calls in the shipyard. A staging collapsed that he was usually first across, and a heavy rivet tool barely missed him when it came crashing down from above. Wolf always wondered if someone had done this deliberately for a number of reasons, not the least being that his first and last names were German.

Wolf's youngest brother, Guenther, sailed on the Liberty Ships back and forth to England as an engineering officer in the merchant marine. These ships were also easy targets for the U-Boats prowling the North Atlantic. Guenther was in London during the Blitz. He married an English woman from Kent by the name of Dorothy. Dorothy was the first of eight wives for Guenther. The family thought he was always searching and compensating for the mother he hadn't met until he was 12 years old. Guenther had the habit of disappearing from contact with the family over the years, only to suddenly reappear.

At one time, the family received a photograph of Guenther at a party with some of the Rockefellers. He wore his merchant marine officer's uniform in the photo. I never learned Guenther's relationship with them. However, remember the Vanderlip family that had commissioned *Boy and Panther* modeled after Wolf? I learned later that the Vanderlips were associated with the Rockefellers through at least one marriage, so it is possible that Wolf introduced his brother to the Vanderlip circle of acquaintances.

In August of 1971, Guenther suddenly appeared at the Robert LaFleur Municipal Airport in Waterville on a commuter flight. He had recently returned from Saigon in South Vietnam, where he had apparently served as a military advisor. The family had not seen or heard from him in years. One of his nephew's security clearances in the army had been affected because the nephew had not listed his uncle in Vietnam at the time of his clearance application—because he hadn't known that Guenther was there.

After World War II, Wolfgang, his current wife, Myrtle, and his former wife, Doris, bought the Preble Studio. They successfully ran the business for over 25 years. During those years, Wolf refused to speak German, pretending to have forgotten it because he was so ashamed of the country he had come from. He never bought on credit and insisted on paying cash for any and all purchases. He was cautious and philosophical about the stock market, blaming the crash on investors buying on margin with money they didn't have. Whenever the Preble Studio was audited, the auditor always complimented him on the accuracy of the books.

Wolf's papers include two personal responses from the director of the Federal Bureau of Investigation, J. Edgar Hoover. The responses are not form letters. Rather, both were typed and personally addressed to Wolf. The signatures on both letters are in ink and are Mr. Hoover's. One of the responses is in regard to a concern Wolf had with a mail fraud incident, and Mr. Hoover referred the case to the U.S. Postal Inspector. The other response is in regard to a concern Wolf had over the growing communist movement in the United States, and some concerns he had about some communist sentiment and sympathy he knew of in Waterville.

Wolf loved democracy. He knew it was very important that the lessons learned from the Nazis' rise to power not be forgotten, lest the terrible history of WW II repeat itself. Mr. Hoover encouraged Wolf to provide any further information related to anti-American matters to the special agent in charge of the FBI's Boston field office.

Wolfgang Egon Weigelt was a patriot who knew the cost of his own freedom and lived every one of his days in thanks for it. He was proud of his citizenship in what he referred to as "the greatest country in the world." He lived at the old house on Winter Street and eventually died there with his family around him on the early morning of December 27, 1983.

Wolf used to comment that, through his friendship with Frank Vanderlip, Jr., and his years on Wall Street working with large sums of money, he had always been close to money, but never had any himself. Wolf was a rich man, however. He was known as a man of honor, strength, and character, and died with these attributes intact. And when he went into eternity, he took these attributes with him. Most importantly, he had a strong faith in the saving power of his Savior, the Lord Jesus Christ. I'm proud to say that Wolfgang E. Weigelt was my father.

Aunt Marion and Debora checking on Ella at the Maine Veterans Cemetery in Augusta. (Photo by Alden Weigelt)

Chapter 12

IS THERE SOMETHING IN THEIR GENETICS?

On August 14, 1928, the Sixteenth Maine Regimental Association held their fifty-third reunion in Waterville. The 16th Maine was the last Civil War unit that John C. Bradbury served in combat with. There was a booklet printed for the reunion that included the treasurer's report, letters from the president and vice presidents of the association, as well as letters of greeting from members who could not attend that year. Members who had passed away the previous year were also remembered in the booklet. John Bradbury would have been one of the old soldiers in attendance.

In the beginning of the booklet is a short essay explaining the significance of the Grand Army of the Republic. I have quoted it just as it was written in the booklet:

The Heritage of the G. A. R.

The Grand Army of the Republic is a unique organization.

No child can be born into it.

No proclamation of President or edict of King or Czar can command admission.

No university or institution of learning can issue a diploma authorizing its holder to entrance.

No act of Congress or Parliament secures recognition.

The wealth of a Vanderbilt cannot purchase the position.

Its doors swing open only on the presentation of the bit of parchment, worn, torn, and begrimed it may be, which certifies to an honorable discharge from the Armies or Navies of the Nation during the War Against the Rebellion.

And, unlike any other organization, no new blood can come in.

There are no growing ranks from which recruits can be drawn into the Grand Army of the Republic. With the consummation of peace through victory its ranks were closed forever.

Its lines are steadily and swiftly growing thinner and the ceaseless tramp of its columns is with ever-lessening tread. The gaps in the picket line grow wider day by day. Details are made for the reserve summoned into the shadowy regions until by and by only a solitary sentinel will stand guard waiting until the bugle call from beyond shall muster out the last comrade of the Grand Army of the Republic.

All the members of the Grand Army of the Republic are gone now, but their spirit lives on in the spirit of today's warrior.

John C. Bradbury had five grandchildren. The eldest, Merle Penney, served in World War I as an officer in the United States Army. A granddaughter, Ella T. Bradbury, served in the United States Army Air Corps during World War II. Ella remained in the service, and when the Air Corps became the United States Air Force, Ella was there. Ella continued to serve in the air force, and retired after more than twenty years of service. Ella's military headstone lists her service as World War II, Korea, and Vietnam. During World War II, Ella served at General Dwight D. Eisenhower's headquarters. Ella often reminded her family that she was with the general for the planning of D-Day in London, and remained with his headquarters as they moved all across Europe until the war was won. She also remarked that she hoped that "the Old Gentleman" would be as proud of her service as she was proud of his.

Ella never married. The service was her home. Ella was born September 6, 1918. She died after living out her retirement at an old soldier's home in Washington, D.C., on Friday, May 26, 2006, three days before Memorial Day and four days before the Decoration Day of the Grand Army of the Republic. As noted earlier, her grandfather, John C. Bradbury, had passed away three days *after* Decoration Day, on June 2, 1931. Ella's closest surviving relative, Marion Jackins, also a granddaughter of John C. Bradbury, received Ella's flag during her military funeral at the Veterans Cemetery in Augusta, Maine. My wife, Debora, had the honor of escorting Aunt Marion to the funeral.

John C. Bradbury had many descendants. On the list is one who served in WW I. One served in WW II, and during Korea and Vietnam. One served in Vietnam. Another served during Vietnam and later served

Ella never married. She dedicated her life to her country and hoped the Old Gentleman would be proud. (Photo by Alden Weigelt)

as a police officer. One is a minister who briefly served as a police officer, and then served in Afghanistan as an army chaplain. One served in the Coast Guard. One served as a firefighter. One served as a marine. Two more served as police officers. These two are father and son and are both married to nurses. One descendant is a teacher who married an Iraq war veteran who is also a teacher. One married an air force fighter pilot, one married a sailor, and one married a minister. More of John's descendants than not have served others and something greater than themselves in some way—or at least married those who did.

The one who married a minister is our youngest daughter, Erica. Erica (Weigelt) Alix married the new minister of our congregation, Blessed Hope Church in Waterville, on December 18, 2010. Reverend Michael Alix moved up to the senior pastor position from the associate pastor position later in 2010, when he was called by the church to do so soon after Dr. Timothy Setzer moved to the senior ministerial position at the Advent Christian Village at Dowling Park, Florida, a retirement community of our denomination.

The one who served in Afghanistan, Captain Earl E. Weigelt, my nephew, is the full-time Family Support Chaplain for the Maine Army National Guard. One of Earl's responsibilities is notifying families of the death of their loved ones. Earl also serves in supporting the families during and after their time of trial, and conducts many of the funerals. Earl served a year in Afghanistan at Kandahar Airfield. He received special recognition for his service as a chaplain, and he was decorated for it.

Earl's son, Kenton Weigelt, is an infantryman in the United States Marine Corps, and, as this book is being written, has been training for deployment to Afghanistan. Kenton's unit will train Afghanistan border security forces. Kenton will not deploy at this time, however. Just before deployment, a medical condition that required surgery, physical therapy, and convalescence was discovered, so he wouldn't be ready to go with his unit. Kenton was heartbroken being left behind. Just before going into surgery, two Marine Corps officers appeared in the pre-op area. They presented and pinned Kenton with his promotion to lance corporal just before he was operated on. Only another warrior truly understands the significance.

William A. Lindie, Jr., Master Sergeant (MSgt.), United States Air Force, Retired, whom you met in Chapter 7, was not the first of his family to serve in the military, nor would he be the last. Lindie's hometown was Monson, Maine. Bill's father, William Lindie Sr., served in World War I with the 22nd Engineers. William Sr. was gassed with mustard gas by the Germans during his combat tour in France fighting in "the war to end all wars."

William Sr.'s brother, Elmer H. Lindie, served as a sniper in Company F, 103rd Infantry Regiment, 26th Division during the Great War. Elmer was recognized for action occurring on the front lines in France in 1918. His citation reads: "The Distinguished Service Cross is presented to Elmer H. Lindie, Private, U.S. Army, for extraordinary heroism in action near Bois-de-St. Remy, France, September 12, 1918. Under heavy grenade and rifle fire, Private Lindie crawled forward from shell hole to shell hole, until he reached a flank position of an enemy machine-gun nest, from which point he killed a gunner and caused the rest to surrender to his comrades. General Orders No. 26 W.D., 1919."

The only decoration that is higher than the Distinguished Service Cross is the Congressional Medal of Honor. Private Lindie also received the Silver Star and the Purple Heart during his combat service, and the French awarded Elmer the prestigious Croix de Guerre for heroism. If you remember the story of Sgt. Alvin York, according to his family, Private Lindie's combat experience and decorations were very similar.

MSgt. Bill Lindie's older brother, Harry Lindie, served in the 25th Tropical Lightning Division in the Pacific during World War II. Harry was at Schofield Barracks at Pearl Harbor the morning of December 7, 1941, during the surprise attack by the Japanese. Harry continued to serve with the 25th all over the Pacific. He was with the invasion to retake the

Philippines later in the war when General Douglas MacArthur kept his promise to return and liberate the Philippine Islands from the Japanese.

Harry Lindie was in the process of stringing communication wire with another soldier when they were jumped by a Japanese patrol. The other soldier was killed and Harry was bayoneted in the abdomen. Harry was able to defend himself with his 1911A1 .45 automatic pistol, and he blew the head off of the soldier who had bayoneted him. Afterwards, Harry discovered that his intestines were outside his body due to the wound. He lay down on the jungle floor and soaked his field jacket in muddy water. He packed his wet field jacket around his own intestines to keep them moist before going into shock and passing out. Harry awoke later in a field hospital. It took him several months in a military hospital in New Zealand to recover.

MSgt. Bill Lindie had an uncle on his mother's side by the name of James Alvah Crockett, his mother's youngest brother. James joined the army air corps during World War II. The Army sent him to flight school, but unfortunately, during his training as a pilot he crashed twice and was washed out. The army then trained James as a bomber navigator and he went to England with the Mighty Eighth Air Force. He flew several combat missions before his aircraft was shot down. James then sat out the remainder of the war as a prisoner in a German Luftwaffe concentration camp.

The American Legion in Monson, Maine, was started by three World War I veterans, including the brothers William Lindie Sr. and Elmer Lindie, as well as another man by the name of Ira Bishop.

Master Sergeant William Lindie had two children who also served in the air force. His oldest child, Debora, chose the civilian profession of nursing, and at this writing, she has served her chosen profession and has put up with and been married to me for 35 years.

Remember Joshua Lawrence Chamberlain, the hero of Gettysburg at Little Round Top? He later became the governor of Maine and won four one-year terms, but that still was not the end of his service. Governor Angus King remembered this example in the Bowdoin College commencement address he gave on May 25, 1996. He told the following story:

Around 1880, there was a contested gubernatorial election. No one knew who had won because of the closeness of the election, and a recount and vote in the Executive Council was called for. While waiting for this to take place, men from the opposing parties fought so hard with each other over the issue that they armed themselves. Someone thought to send for the former governor, General Chamberlain, who was then serving as president of Bowdoin College. Chamberlain rode to the State House and locked himself alone inside the building. He took the position that the only way to solve the dilemma was to allow the State Supreme Court to decide the matter. The parties demonstrated around Augusta with torchlight parades. A sniper was even reported to have been on the dome of the State House.

Finally, an armed mob decided to storm the State House where Joshua Chamberlain had locked himself in, and there were calls to kill Chamberlain. Chamberlain opened the door and came out on the steps. The crowd quieted down. Chamberlain addressed the crowd: "I am here to see that the laws of the State of Maine are fully and fairly executed. If any man wants to kill me for it, here I am."

After about twenty seconds passed, the voice of an old man came from the back of the crowd. He said, "I was with you at Little Round Top, General, and if one of these ruffians touches a hair on your head, he'll have to answer to me." The dispute and the crisis ended then.

Many of the people we have spoken of have gone on to serve others and society in different ways. I can remember as a kid that most of the Waterville Police Department officers were World War II veterans. When I first entered the police service in the 1970s, some of the WW II veterans were still around, but Korean War and Vietnam veterans were serving as cops, too.

Russell LeBlanc was a neighbor, and had lived just four doors down the street on Winter Street. Russell had served in the 1st Infantry Division during World War II and had landed on Omaha Beach with the division's 7th Field Artillery the morning of June 6, 1944, in Normandy, France. Russell came home from World War II and worked the rest of his life as a Waterville police officer. The kids in the city nicknamed him "Casey the Cop." Russell's wife, Joan, served for many years as the Clerk of Court for the Waterville District Court. Their oldest daughter, Ann, became a psychologist and eventually served the State of Maine as Chief Forensic Psychologist.

Louis Simon served in the army in World War II with his two brothers. Louis's brother, Simon Simon, also served in the army, and their other brother, Moses Simon, served in the army air force. Louis was taken prisoner by the Germans. All three brothers received the Purple Heart for being wounded in combat, according to the memorial stone placed for them at the Central Maine Veterans Memorial Park in Winslow. Louis returned home after World War II and joined the Waterville Police Department, where he eventually retired after many years as the patrol captain of the department.

I am forever grateful for knowing him and counting him as my friend. (Photo by Alden Weigelt)

Now retired, Waterville Police Officer Malcolm Charles served in Vietnam in the United States Marine Corps, as did retired Detective Harold (Dusty) Woodside. Dusty was wounded in Vietnam. His dad, Phillip Woodside, had served as a navy corpsman during World War II. Dusty joined and then served until his retirement as a respected officer of the Waterville Police Department. After retiring as a detective, he joined the Oakland Police Department, where he continues to serve today as a school resource officer.

Dusty's mother, Lucille Woodside, was a registered nurse and served others all of her professional life at Thayer Hospital. Dusty's brother, John Woodside, followed his mother into nursing, and has dedicated his life to serving others at the same hospital. Dusty even married a nurse. His wife, Linda, is a nurse as well as a social worker, and of her five brothers, three served in the military during Vietnam.

I had the privilege of working with Michael K. Hross when I worked for the Oakland Police Department prior to joining Waterville PD. Mike was a retired New York City police officer. Before Mike became a cop, he served two tours as a marine in Vietnam. After he retired from NYPD, he brought his family to Maine. Mike worked for the Waterville Police Department for a couple of years before joining the Oakland Police Department where I met him. Mike had remained in the military after

Vietnam, serving first in the Marine Corps Reserves and later in the Air Force Reserves.

Mike left full-time police work in June of 2000 to serve once again in the military full-time. This time it would be as a member of the new National Guard Civil Support Team based in Waterville. The mission of the team is to respond to incidents suspected to involve weapons of mass destruction (WMDs). The teams were formed across the country prior to September 11, 2001, and the brand-new Civil Support WMD Team for the State of Maine was formed and based in Waterville near the National Guard Armory. Mike was one of the original "plank owners" of the unit.

In February of 2004, Mike was diagnosed with cancer. He passed away in 2005 after a long battle with his illness, about a month before he would have turned 57 years old. He left behind a wife and three sons who loved him dearly. Mike was a man of character and honor, and he was one of the finest warriors I have ever known. I am forever grateful for having the privilege to know him and count him as my friend.

When I came to the Waterville Police Department in January 2007, John Morris was the Chief of Police of Waterville. It was John who hired me. He had served a 30-year career in the United States Navy, retiring as a captain before entering law enforcement here in Maine. John first served as Chief of Police of Richmond before coming to Waterville. In addition to attaining the rank of captain in the navy, John had also captained his own ship, the USS *Cayuga* (LST-1186). John retired from Waterville in 2007, but came out of retirement once again in 2011 to serve as the Commissioner of Public Safety for the State of Maine under Governor Paul LePage.

Dr. Joseph A. Marshall had a private practice in Waterville. Dr. Marshall was also the Scott Paper Company plant physician in Winslow where Larry LaMarre and Frank Siviski of Chapter 4 worked. Joe Marshall served in World War II as a navy corpsman, which means he was an enlisted man and a medic. Dr. Joseph Marshall returned to the navy during the Korean War as an officer and a doctor.

Real Cyr also worked for Scott Paper Company as an electrician, and worked for Larry LaMarre at the mill. Real had served in the submarine service in the navy during World War II. He was also a Navy Commando as well as having been a POW. Real's son, Andy Cyr, followed in his father's footsteps and joined the navy. Andy graduated as an officer from the U.S. Naval Academy at Annapolis, Maryland. After his time in the navy, Andy continued to serve the community as a high school math teacher.

Of Larry LaMarre's two children, both entered professions serving others. Kevin went into the ministry and his sister Tia went into nursing.

A man I know from church, Kenneth Bernard, also served in the United States Navy. Ken's specialty was in communications. He served two years in London, England, at the Navy Headquarters/European and Mediterranean Command, located next door to the United States Embassy in the 1950s. Ken finished his enlistment on board the USS *Providence*, a guided missile light cruiser. Following a discharge from the regular navy, Ken enlisted in the United States Navy Reserve and served 19 years in addition to his active-duty years in the regular navy. Ken was second generation Navy. His dad, George Bernard, had served in the navy during World War II. George served in the South Atlantic aboard a mine sweeper, the USS *Magnet*, protecting our convoys.

Another man I know from church, Estol R. (Mack) McClintock, served in the army in World War II and continued in the army, completing a full career and retiring as a command sergeant major more than 24 years later. Mack's childhood sweetheart, Emaline, served in the United States Navy in Washington, D.C., during the war. They married after Mack returned and they were reunited.

Mack had enlisted in the 1st Infantry Division, known as The Big Red One, the same division his father had served in France during World War I. Mack's brother served in the 17th Airborne Division during World War II.. After finally retiring in 1967 and moving to Maine, Mack dedicated the rest of his life to the service of other veterans. He served many years as a member of the Veteran's Advisory Board under the direction of the Department of Defense. Mack later became one of the founding board members of the Martin's Point Health Care System, which is dedicated to serving veterans and their families with affordable health care.

It comes down to this: there are those who serve others and then there are the others. The ones who continue to serve are the soldiers, cops, firemen, EMTs, nurses, doctors, clergy, teachers, some politicians, and anyone else who chooses a profession that serves something greater than themselves for the benefit of others. These people are the glue that holds our society together. Without them civilization would fall apart.

The others include all the citizens of our great nation. These are the people who contribute in many different ways to society and those who don't because they can't. There are those that are old, and those that are young. Some are healthy and some are infirm. Some are weak and some are strong. Some are productive and some are not. Some are frightened. But they all have one thing in common: they are loved by those who have dedicated their lives by choosing to serve that something greater than themselves and for the benefit of others.

On October 4, 2008, United States Army Lieutenant Colonel David Grossman, Retired, came to Blessed Hope Church in Waterville to address the law enforcement officers of the State of Maine. Grossman had by this time come to the state several times to speak with deploying National Guard troops going into harm's way. Army National Guard Chaplain Captain Earl Weigelt had worked with Major General John Libby, the commander of the Maine National Guard, in bringing Grossman to Maine for the soldiers.

Colonel Grossman is a former U.S. Army Ranger and West Point instructor who is currently an author, lecturer, and trainer. Colonel Grossman has written on a variety of subjects that include the physiological and psychological effects of combat, media influence on violence, and how to mentally prepare for combat exposure. He lectures on how to emotionally survive combat, as well as on how to avoid or recover from post-traumatic stress disorder (PTSD). Colonel Grossman's works include *On Killing* and *On Combat.*

The people of Blessed Hope Church wanted to give law enforcement in Maine the gift of Colonel Grossman's message on the warrior mindset and what Grossman has termed the "Bullet-Proof Mind." The Waterville Police Department helped the church organize the event. The people of the church hosted and paid for it. Colonel Grossman spoke to law enforcement on Saturday and then on Sunday spoke to the congregation on the topic of desensitizing our kids through media violence.

As both a member of Blessed Hope Church and an officer of the Waterville Police Department, I worked with Dr. Timothy Setzer, then Senior Pastor of Blessed Hope Church, and with Deputy Police Chief Charles Rumsey of Waterville PD in planning the event. While I was helping coordinate our event, I received a call from the Boston unit of the United States Air Force Office of Special Investigations (OSI). A few of the special agents from that unit had just returned from a combat tour in the Middle East. The agent who contacted me told me that one of her colleagues was having a hard time with what he had experienced over there. She said that she knew of Colonel Grossman's work and thought that the agent needed to hear his message. She wanted to know if they could come.

Of course they could come. The three agents from the air force's OSI received a standing ovation from all the police officers and military personnel in attendance the day of the event. And those present would remember and "validate the sacrifice" of those who have given and those who have given all.

Those who give to their community, to their country, even give their all to something greater than themselves are, I believe, a special type of person. Not everyone rises to the challenge. Many understandably fulfill the role of the "protected" as they go about the everyday tasks of sustaining a civilization. Then there are the predators among us that the protectors take to task. Predators can include criminals, terrorists, hostile countries, oppressive ideologies, and even disease or social ills.

Lt. Colonel Grossman uses the metaphor of sheep, wolves and the sheepdog to explain this concept. The sheep are the good and gentle people of society who would never intentionally hurt another human being. The wolves are the evil persons who prey upon the sheep. The sheepdogs are those who watch over, protect, and guide the sheep. Soldiers and cops are given the metaphor of warrior-sheepdogs.

The warrior role is unique, as the warrior risks life and limb to protect, to serve, to sacrifice. I believe that the warrior role is a noble calling likened to that of a minister, nurse, or doctor. The test of a calling means that the one called can never be fulfilled doing anything else. I believe and acknowledge that some callings may not necessarily be forever and that callings can change. The secret is in knowing when the calling has changed and to be ready to move on to the next one.

The people I have sought to honor and recognize in this book may not still be serving in a warrior role, but at the time of their service they belonged to the warrior community. The job may have changed, but in their heart of hearts they are still warriors. Is it something in their genetics? Well, at least it seems that certain personalities are more drawn to certain professions than are other personalities. But there is no denying that not just anyone can be a warrior, and the ones that are...are special.

The Grand Army of the Republic has long since faded away. The memories of their members are inspirational and precious, and should never be forgotten. Thankfully their spirit still lives on in the hearts of the warriors who have followed. As American citizens, it is our responsibility to realize and recognize our debt to our noble warriors. As Colonel Grossman reminds us: we should live each day of our lives worthy of their sacrifice.

Chapter 13

BLESSED HOPE CHURCH, 10 PLEASANT STREET, WATERVILLE, ME 04901

The afternoon of May 28, 2011, the Saturday of Memorial Day weekend, Debora and I were on our way to Wellington, Maine, to visit with our friends Mack and Emaline McClintock. Mack and Emaline are former members of our church. Mack and I had served together on the Board of Deacons for several years, and Emaline had sometimes played the piano during the church services at Blessed Hope Church in Waterville.

As the McClintocks aged, it became more and more difficult for them to travel the 46 miles every week, so some years ago, they began attending a church closer to home. Mack had retired from the United States Army after more than 24 years of service. He served in combat during World War II and then remained in the service until he retired in 1967 and moved to Maine. Mack is 88 now.

I started serving as a deacon in 1987 with several other men of the church, including George Brown and Neil Gibbs. A few years later, Mack McClintock was asked to join the deacons as well. Neil, George, and Mack were all army veterans who had served during WW II. George and Mack had served in the combat theater overseas. There were other men in the church who had also served, but at the time, I was closest to these three.

When socializing at church functions, these guys were just as outgoing as anyone else; whether speaking with another veteran or another member of the congregation, it made no difference. But when they worked together with the other deacons on a project or at a meeting, there seemed to be a special bond between the three, and that would sometimes come out in a comment here or there. In regard to their comments to each other, I would just listen. The bond between them seemed to be more than the result of their service to the church congregation or the deacon board. They never bragged about their service to their country and rarely mentioned it. They did not set themselves apart from others in the congregation or neglect them in any way. As a matter of fact, they were some of the most dedicated men on the board when it came to ministering to others.

George Brown and I became good friends over the years, and we often met for coffee together at Jorgensen's on Main Street in Waterville. We spoke of spiritual matters and theology, and George was somewhat of a mentor to me in regard to my Christian faith. In addition to our talks on biblical and church matters, George told me a little about his service in the army.

George married his wife of more than 50 years, Phyllis, in September of 1942. In November of that year, George entered military service in the army, receiving an assignment to the Signal Corps. George served in North Africa, Corsica, and Italy until August of 1945, when his unit was ordered to the Pacific to continue fighting the Japanese after the war in Europe was won. George was on a troop ship heading to the Pacific when the ship made a sudden change in course and headed for New York City. It was announced to the troops on the ship that a new kind of weapon had been dropped on Japan, that the Japanese were going to surrender, and that they had been ordered home. George and Phyllis had been married for only two months before he shipped out, and they had not seen each other for three years before finally reuniting after the war was over.

George retired from the phone company and his son, Steve Brown, in later years served as the pastor of Blessed Hope Church. George had served in the positions of deacon and elder while at the church before his son took over as pastor. When his son started serving as associate pastor, George stepped down as elder so as not to create a conflict of interest. Steve eventually served as senior pastor until he later moved on with his wife Lavonne to help start the Berkshire Institute for Christian Studies in Western Massachusetts.

George still served as a deacon while his son was at Blessed Hope, and he continued to serve under the new pastor for a few more years. George and Phyllis moved to a retirement community in southern Vermont a couple of years after his son left. They sold their house on Collette Street in Waterville and moved to Vermont to be a little closer to their only son, who was living in Western Massachusetts. Shortly after moving to Vermont, and just before they were to travel to Massachusetts for the wedding of their only granddaughter, Phyllis passed away suddenly at their home. George later remarried a widow by the name of Beatrice, whom he met at the retirement home. Bea's first husband had been a career army officer and had also served during World War II.

George often told me how different the nation was back then, during the war years. He reminisced about how the nation pulled together and how everyone did their part. And George also reminded me that when he went to war, he had to leave his new bride for three years before seeing her again, and how he was forever grateful that he had returned while so many others hadn't. George had seen the cost of combat and war, but would only speak of those experiences in the safety of others like himself.

Shortly after George left Blessed Hope, Mack also left. Neil Gibbs served a little longer and then stepped down from the Board of Deacons. Neil passed away a few years ago. After a reorganization of church government, I served with Neil's son, David Gibbs, on the Board of Elders.

David had retired from UPS, where he worked most of his life after returning from Vietnam. I am fortunate to consider Dave Gibbs as my close friend, and still serve with him on the Board of Elders. Years after George Brown moved to Vermont, Dave and I developed a similar relationship based on our commonality and beliefs in spiritual matters and theology. David was in the army and went to Vietnam in 1966. Dave remembers well the turmoil that the country was in during those years, and how it was different from the years that Neil Gibbs and George Brown had served.

David served a year in Vietnam as a courier carrying classified documents and reports, and flew in about every type of aircraft that we had over there. He also helped defend the perimeter of the bases he was assigned to when they came under attack, as they often did. When his year was up, he was sent back to the States. David remarked that it was not a direct flight on his trip back home to the "world," and that he had to change planes a couple of times. He remembered that there was a young soldier on the plane to Hawaii who was going there for his scheduled R&R. David told of the other soldiers on the plane learning that the young soldier was married but could not afford to fly his wife to Hawaii to meet him, so he was going to spend his leave time alone without her. Dave said that the rest of the soldiers took up a collection, and the married soldier called his wife and got her to Hawaii with the help of the donations of other soldiers. Dave stated that this generosity was not uncommon between soldiers, even soldiers who did not know each other. And that's the way it is. Away from home and in harm's way, in the end warriors only have each other.

Elwood Ellis, another elder at my church, also served in Vietnam. Elwood was a marine. Elwood survived the war and returned home to raise a family of three girls and one boy. He owns his own surveying business now. He continued to serve others in the church as well as in public office as a member of the school board and the board of selectmen in the town of China.

Another man I served with at the church for many years, Tom Cunningham, was a school teacher and assistant principal. Tom's father and longtime member of the church, Ken Cunningham, served in the Marine Corps during World War II, and saw action in the Pacific. Ken and his wife, Rachel, raised seven children and now have twenty grandchildren. Ken celebrated the Maine outdoors as an avid hunter and fisherman all his life. Ken belonged to that special group of men in the church who had answered the call and came from the Greatest Generation to serve their country during one of the most desperate times in the history of the world. And he would be another member of that special generation who returned to work and raise a family. Ken worked many years at the Harris Baking Company in Waterville to put food on the table for his wife and seven kids. Ken passed away during the summer of 2010, and as this book is written, his wife Rachel is the oldest living member of Blessed Hope Church.

Another member of Blessed Hope, Arnold Carter, attended Berkshire Christian College, as he had considered becoming a minister. He served in Korea as an army medic in a field hospital as that war drew to a close. Two of Arnold's older brothers had served in combat in the army during World War II, and had both survived the war. Another member, Michael Craig, served in the Marine Corps as a drill instructor, and his father, Cecil, had served a combat tour in Vietnam, also as a marine.

Rick Olin and his family attended the church during the late 1980s and early 1990s. Rick was a staff manager at Scott Paper Company in Winslow. He had three daughters and a son who was the youngest of his four kids. Our son, Shawn, was friends with his son, Jeff.

Rick served in the navy during the Vietnam War as an aviator and an officer. He flew as the Radar Intercept Officer (RIO) in the famous F-4 Phantom with VF-111, the "Sundowners." Lieutenant JG (Junior Grade) Rick Olin, United States Naval Reserve, flew more than 140 combat missions over North and South Vietnam. He acknowledges the supernatural hand of our Lord in his being here today.

Rick and I often talked about aviation, as he was aware that I was a pilot. One day, Rick mentioned the concern aviators have at hearing sound or experiencing vibration that we suspect is not normal for our aircraft. Rick told me to imagine those concerns when you were "feet dry" and knew the "Indians" on the ground were not friendly.

When I met Rick, America was involved in the first Gulf War. There had been a TV news special on emergency combat field repair of aircraft filmed at the military school that taught this skill. The school used the now-aging F-4 for training, and one of the repairs demonstrated used a cut-out coffee can as a patch with hose clamps on the large hydraulic line that runs atop the aircraft along the fuselage. I was amazed at this repair and later asked Rick about it. He told me that on the aircraft carrier he served on with the Sundowners, the crew chiefs of the maintenance crews were qualified in the Phantom's ejection seat. He explained that if a crew chief certified an aircraft as airworthy, but the pilot doubted it, the pilot could require the crew chief to ride with him on a test flight. In other words, put your money where your mouth is.

During that same conversation, Rick's face got a little dark. He went on to tell me he once saw an F-4 come aboard one day and, after they got the injured RIO out of the back seat, they shoved the 2.4-million-dollar fighter over the side. It was beyond repair...but it had brought its crew home.

On March 6, 1972, Rick was flying in his role as RIO with his pilot, Jim Stillinger, as the lead element of a two-aircraft flight of F-4B Phantoms of VF-111. The flight was over the Gulf of Tonkin, east of North Vietnam. The flight was vectored to intercept North Vietnamese MIG-17s that were flying south in an attempt to intercept incoming American aircraft. As RIO, part of Rick's job was to work the intercept solution to engage the enemy MIGs. Stillinger engaged one of the more maneuverable MIGs, while his wingman pilot, Garry Weigand, and his RIO, Bill Freckleton, maneuvered to cover Stillinger and Rick. Stillinger pushed the attack, but from his position could not get a missile lock and advised Weigand to take the shot if he could. Weigand fired a Sidewinder up the tailpipe of the MIG-17.

This victory was the second MIG kill in the history of VF-111 in Vietnam. Lt. JG Rick Olin received the Distinguished Flying Cross for "Heroism in Aerial Flight on 6 March 1972." The Distinguished Flying Cross is between the Silver Star and the Bronze Star in order of precedence. This award is given for combat or noncombat acts of distinction in flight. Rick and his wife have now retired to Florida, where Rick volunteers at the Museum of Naval Aviation at Pensacola. He continues to fuel his love for the navy and its rich history.

Brian Wedge, spoken of in Chapter 8, was at school at Nyack College with our daughter Megan on September 11, 2001. Both Brian and Megan were studying to be teachers. They had chosen to attend Nyack College because of their Christian faith. Brian was going to college with the help that he had received from the army while serving in the Army Reserve.

Brian's Army Reserve unit was mobilized shortly after 9/11, and his unit—elements of the 325th Military Intelligence Battalion—spent a year at Fort Bragg backfilling the 82nd Airborne Division that deployed to Afghanistan right after the attacks on our country. A year later, Brian's unit returned home and he returned to Nyack for the fall semester of 2002.

Brian and Megan became engaged while Brian was on leave that summer of 2002. His unit mobilized again in February of 2003, and this time the unit was combined with the 205th Military Intelligence Brigade and participated in the invasion of Iraq that March. Brian remained in Iraq until the following Christmas. The maple tree on the front lawn of our home had a yellow ribbon around it for that period of time. Several other trees in the neighborhood had yellow ribbons as well, symbolizing the hope of a safe return for a loved one.

Brian's unit was headquartered at a captured Iraqi airbase at Balad, outside of Baghdad. One of Brian's friends was killed when an improvised explosive device (IED) destroyed his Humvee. Brian's job was radio repair and care of classified communication equipment, and he had to remove the classified radio equipment, with his friend's blood still on it, from the demolished vehicle his friend had died in.

Brian also traveled in convoys to support the mission of the military intelligence unit at other bases, including Baghdad International Airport. While in transit one day, an insurgent appeared with a rocket-propelled grenade (RPG) and sighted in on Brian's convoy after just having fired a round that missed. Another friend, providing security directly behind Brian's vehicle in the rear security Humvee, opened up on the insurgent with his Mark 19 grenade launcher from the turret of his vehicle and eliminated the threat, or sent him straight to his maker, whichever you prefer.

Fortunately, Brian would come home one day and marry Megan. Today, Brian and Megan both serve in their chosen profession of teaching. Sergeant First Class (SFC) Brian Wedge also continues to serve his country in the Army Reserve.

My nephew, Earl Weigelt, was the associate pastor of Blessed Hope for nine years. In addition to being an associate pastor, he worked with the youth of the church. Earl completed his doctor of divinity degree at Gordon-Conwell Theological Seminary while serving at Blessed Hope. After he received his doctorate, he wrestled with where he believed he was being called to serve next. A short time later, Earl joined the Maine Army National Guard as a chaplain.

Chaplain Captain Weigelt is the fulltime Family Support Chaplain for the Maine Army National Guard. Part of his responsibility is making the notifications to next of kin of the death of their loved one, not only for Guard personnel, but for other branches of service as well. He has done many of the funerals too. And there have been a lot of notifications. If you remember the "Dirigo" "I Lead" lesson from Chapter 2, Maine has one of the highest ratios of citizen soldiers serving at this time in our history, just as we did during the Civil War.

In early 2009, Captain Weigelt deployed to Afghanistan and served a year with the headquarters unit of the 286th Combat Sustainment Support Battalion at Kandahar Airfield. Kandahar Airfield is the major allied base of all forces operating in southern Afghanistan. All troops and supplies come through Kandahar. Earl went out each morning and laid hands and prayed over the trucks of the convoys before they left with their soldiers and cargo on their way to the remote regions of allied control. They were attacked as well. After one such attack and firefight that lasted all day, the soldiers, some of whom had found the Captain's daily ritual amusing, insisted that "Chappy" lay hands on their vehicles, too.

And there were the ramp ceremonies that could come at any time of day. Whenever a soldier killed in action was sent home from Kandahar Airfield, the troops would turn out to pay honor to the sacrifice of the warrior who had given "the most that man can give: life itself...for the sacred cause of justice and the freedom of the world." It didn't matter if the soldier lost was American, Canadian, British, or Australian, everyone turned out. All the allies were there. And Earl remembered that whenever the command sergeant majors of the British or Canadians called their troops to attention, there was something stirring in the way that it was done.

I remember later, after Earl returned home, sharing a video with him of the Remembrance Ceremony that Debora and I had attended in London in November of 2010. When the British sergeant major ordered the Guards to attention and the troops responded in the special way they do, Earl was startled. He told me he was suddenly reminded of the ramp ceremonies in Kandahar. Earl told me that for a moment, he was there again. And it was then that he told me how many ramp ceremonies there had been.

One of the 286th's convoys was attacked in the mountains after dropping their cargo and beginning the long journey back to Kandahar. It was an organized attack, and the enemy had the convoy bracketed with accurate mortar, machine-gun, and small-arms fire. The battle went on for most of the day. Air support came in the form of the air force A-10 Thunderbolt II, or, as it is fondly called, the "Warthog."

That evening, the commanding officer of the 286th, Lt. Colonel Diane Dunn, Command Sergeant Major Peter Barrett, and Captain Earl Weigelt flew out by helicopter to the location of the convoy and battle. They flew to the post-ambush rendezvous point, Camp Frontenac, and met the tired and battle-weary soldiers there. Lt. Colonel Dunn, CSM Barrett, and Captain Weigelt remained with the ambushed troops until the next morning and until they were safely convoyed back to Kandahar Airfield.

Miraculously, no American soldiers were killed, although two were injured seriously enough to require evacuation from the theater. The same could not be said for the enemy. The soldiers were exhausted and dehydrated from the battle and many of them had to have IV fluids administered before they were able to leave the battlefield area. And Captain Weigelt continued to minister to the troops there and during the days that followed back at Kandahar.

On another occasion, Earl and his chaplain assistant went to a remote forward firebase that had experienced an attack a short time before, resulting in wounded American soldiers. A chaplain is considered a noncombatant and is provided with a chaplain assistant. That person serves with the chaplain in his duties, but is not a noncombatant. One of the assistant's critical roles is to protect the chaplain.

One of the things that the soldiers at the firebase seemed to need was rest, and they hadn't gotten a lot lately. The noncombatant chaplain and his chaplain assistant as a team pulled a shift of night guard duty to relieve the soldiers, allowing two more soldiers to get some sleep. These soldiers were suffering the loss of their wounded comrades, as well as experiencing their own physical and emotional exhaustion. Earl contacted Dave Grossman and a few weeks later the colonel's book, *On Combat*, was in the hands of these guys thanks to the chaplain and Colonel Grossman.

Earl returned to the United States with the rest of the 286th after their year in Afghanistan. The unit returned home without having lost a single soldier. Captain Weigelt later received the Bronze Star for his service to his country while in Afghanistan. Earl had mixed emotions about the decoration, as he told me that many of those who receive it have been wounded in actual combat. He also told me that the usual way a chaplain receives this award is with a Purple Heart, both awarded together, posthumously.

Chapter 14

VALOR REMEMBERED AND SERGEANT MACK

On May 28, 2011, Deb and I were almost at Mack and Emaline's home when I thought about the last time we had seen them, a little over a year before. Mack has a bad back and both knees are shot, but the doctors won't operate on him because he also has a bad heart. Mack loves his vegetable garden, which occupies him most of the summer, and he deals with his constant pain.

When we arrived, we found Mack and Emaline just as we remembered them. They are wonderful people and full of life. Mack is a kind and generous man. He is short in stature, but you never picture him in your mind as a short man. Mack is also tough as nails. One of the reasons for our visit was to confirm what I remembered of his service. Accuracy is paramount in recounting the lives of these special people. Emaline and Deb sat down in one part of the living room and caught up on all that had happened since we'd last seen each other. Mack and I sat down on the other side of the room and spoke together.

During a previous visit, Mack had mentioned only two awards. These were a Purple Heart he'd received during WW II, though he was wounded on three separate occasions, and a State of Maine Silver Star that he'd received from Governor John Baldacci. The governor started awarding the State of Maine Silver Star a few years ago in recognition of our Maine veterans.

Though Mack had shared with me the history of his WW II experience, he'd never mentioned any other decorations. From our prior conversations about his combat experience, I knew Mack was a modest man, and before we came for this visit, I did a little research and located acknowledgments on the Home for Heroes website for two Silver Stars that Estol McClintock had also received. One was issued in 1943 and the other in 1945.

I spoke with Mack, confirming what I remembered and learning even more. Mack had enlisted in the 1st Infantry Division during World War II, just as his father had in World War I. Mack's brother enlisted in the 17th Airborne. Mack was part of the first amphibious invasion of North Africa during Operation Torch in November of 1942. His company was in the first wave of attack and was the first on the beach. He was part of a mortar squad, and later, as a sergeant, commanded the squad. Mack was almost taken prisoner by the Germans at one point while covering the withdrawal of the other troops. On another occasion, he was again covering the withdrawal of the rest of his squad when his position took a direct mortar hit. When Mack woke up, he found a piece of shrapnel sticking out of his left shin.

In the hospital, it was found that the piece of hot steel had gone into the bone, and the tip of the metal end had split in two. Both ends of the steel had curved into the shape of a fishhook. The doctors could not remove it from the bone and cut off the protruding metal instead. While in the field hospital, the surgeons decided to evacuate Mack to another hospital where they could cut out that section of bone, which would shorten his left leg a little.

Mack was not having any of this and went AWOL (Absent Without Leave) from the hospital. He was afraid he would become a replacement and not be reunited with his unit. Besides, he didn't much like the idea of a left leg "a little shorter" than the right. Mack hitchhiked back to the front lines. He told me that if a soldier hitchhiked *away* from the front, no one would pick him up. However, as he was headed *toward* the front lines, it was easy to get a ride.

When Mack arrived back with his unit, he had already been reported as AWOL, but his commander took pity on him and let him stay. He had to make frequent trips to the aid station, though, to have the infection that he contracted treated. Mack received his one and only Purple Heart for this wound, as the 1st Infantry had a rule to only give this award to wounded soldiers who were hospitalized. Mack still has the shrapnel in his left shin today.

In July 1943, The Big Red One, as the 1st Infantry Division was referred to because of the red numeral 1 in the division patch, took part in the invasion of Sicily. Once again, Mack was in the first wave of the amphibious invasion. It was in Sicily that Mack had a piece of shrapnel go through the lobe of his right ear. If his head had been turned to the side, it would have gone into his brain. After Sicily, Mack went to England with the 1st Infantry to prepare for the invasion of Fortress Europe.

Mack recalled that when he originally left the States, at the beginning of the war, he traveled to England on the same *Queen Mary* that Norman McKinstry had traveled on after the great ocean liner was converted to a troop ship. The *Queen Mary* was fast, and she traveled without escort due to her superior speed, which also gave her an advantage over the German subs that were trying to score a kill.

When D-Day came, Mack's company was scheduled to land on Omaha Beach in Normandy in the third wave, as his company had been first in the prior two invasions. On the morning of June 6, 1944, Sgt. Mack boarded his landing craft with his 81mm mortar and took his position in the rear. His destination was on the Easy Red Sector of Omaha Beach with the rest of the 16th Regiment of the 1st Infantry Division. Mack's company was right behind the first and second waves, and when his company arrived, the beach was still not secure. Most of those in the first two waves were dead.

Mack was in the rear of the landing craft near the helmsman and boatswain's mate. With him were two replacement lieutenants to provide leadership, as many of the officers in the first two waves were expected to be dead. Sgt. Mack and the lieutenants were also required to push any man that froze in front of them off the craft.

It had been planned for the first wave to land at low tide, and by the time the third wave got close to shore, the tide had started to come in. Mack's landing craft came against a now-submerged obstacle, which tore a hole in the craft and they started to sink. Sgt. Mack ordered the ramp lowered and the men off the boat. As they started to disembark, a mortar round landed in the water behind the stern of the landing craft, killing both of the crewmembers. Mack went back and checked on them before he left the craft. He confirmed that they were both dead.

Mack jumped off the craft into water over his head. His feet got tangled in the barbed wire on the submerged beach, but he managed to make it to shore with his mortar. He set up his mortar with the help of two other soldiers, one with the base plate and one with the bipod. The three men took heavy machine-gun fire from the bluffs, and Mack credits Almighty God with sparing his life. Those on the beach had not yet breached the minefield protecting the seawall and the bluffs, so Mack set the mortar for almost zero trajectory and started dropping rounds into the minefield, successively dropping each one a little farther inland to create a path for the troops through the minefield.

Before Mack left the beach, he dropped his M-1 carbine next to a dead corporal and took the corporal's 1911A1 .45 ACP pistol and belt. Mack carried that pistol as his personal defensive weapon for the rest of the war. Mack explained that the pistol was much more convenient than the rifle while carrying a heavy mortar. Mack remained with the 16th Regiment of the 1st Infantry for the remainder of the war.

I later asked Mack about the two Silver Stars. He said he had been nominated for the Distinguished Service Cross for what he did on Omaha Beach, but it had been downgraded to a Silver Star, which he received for the action later in 1945.

During the Battle of the Bulge in January 1945, Mack knew his brother was serving a short distance away with the 17th Airborne. When the fighting started to die down, Mack got permission to travel to his brother's unit to visit him. When he arrived, he learned that his brother had been killed the week before. The lieutenant told Mack that as his brother advanced across a field, a shell hit just in front of him, killing him instantly with a piece of shrapnel that went up through his chin and out the top of his head.

After that, Mack's parents obtained a Congressional Order to bring Mack home, as he was the only surviving son. Mack refused the order. He also refused several attempts by his commanders to make him an officer by means of a battlefield commission. Mack explained that, if he had accepted the commission, he would have had to leave his men because the army would not have allowed him to command the men he had soldiered with all this time. Mack would not leave his men.

He was wounded once again in early 1945 during another artillery attack. This time, he received a piece of shrapnel near his groin. He had been trying to deliver a message up a road the Germans had zeroed. Mack left his Jeep and driver behind and walked up the road. The next thing he knew, he woke up in the woods near the side of the road, as he had been blown over the ditch beside it. After he woke up, he pulled the piece of shrapnel out. Mack remarked that it barely missed the "family jewels."

Mack continued to lead his men through France, Belgium, Germany, and Czechoslovakia until victory in Europe on May 8, 1945.

He returned to service in 1948 and pursued a career in the army until he retired in 1967. Mack retired as a command sergeant major and a captain in the reserves. He served at Fort Myer in Arlington, Virginia, with the 3rd Infantry, also known as the "Old Guard" and "Escort to the President of the United States." Mack met General, and then President, Dwight David Eisenhower twice. The first time was when the general met the troops prior to D-Day. The second time was when, as president of the United States, Eisenhower responded to a simulation of a nuclear attack at the secure area under Mack's command.

I again asked Mack about the two Silver Stars. And, as already mentioned, he acknowledged that one was for what he did in Normandy. He was very vague about the other. By way of explanation, he said only that "those things" were issued months later for the "stuff" that had happened months before. (I consider this response a silent reminder of a different sort.)

Mack gave me a typed synopsis of his military service. He received the Silver Star with Oak Leaf Cluster (meaning he received the decoration twice). He received the Bronze Star with two Oak Leaf Clusters (meaning that he received the decoration three times). He received one Purple Heart (but we know he was combat wounded three times). He received the French Fourragère, as well as the Belgian Fourragère, a Combat Infantryman Badge, and several others.

When asked about his service on Omaha Beach, Command Sergeant Major Estol R. McClintock, United States Army, Retired, will tell you that he didn't do all that much. Command Sergeant Major McClintock will tell you that the real heroes are the ones who died there and never came home.

Chapter 15

A NEIGHBOR AT 2 PLEASANT STREET

Sunday, May 16, 2010, was a beautiful spring day. The morning worship service at Blessed Hope was at the usual time of 10:45 A.M., and Pastor Tim Setzer officiated as usual. This was to be one of the last sermons that Tim made at Blessed Hope, as he had recently accepted the position of senior pastor at the Advent Christian Retirement Village at Dowling Park, Florida. Tim planned to leave with his wife, Holly, and son, Caleb, at the end of the following week to begin the new chapter of his ministry at Dowling Park. This was a bittersweet day for a variety of reasons. Tim had served as the pastor of the church for 18 years, ever since arriving in Waterville in 1992, and this afternoon, Tim would also be ministering at a funeral at Blessed Hope.

Blessed Hope Church has been a congregation at this location in Waterville for 115 years. The congregation celebrated its centennial in 1996. The old church, located at the corner of Pearl and Nudd Streets, was torn down in the late 1970s when the new church was built at the other end of the property on Pleasant Street. One of the old parsonages was located at 9 Crommett Street. When Tim came to Waterville, he lived first at the Crommett Street property and then moved to the other parsonage located at 13 Ursula Street. Tim and his wife bought the Ursula Street property from the church and made some renovations to it. When Earl Weigelt, his wife, Carol, and their son, Kenton, came to Waterville in 1994 to minister at Blessed Hope, they lived at the Crommett Street property for several years before it was finally torn down to make room for the new Family Life Center.

Next to the church, at 2 Pleasant Street, is the home of Dr. Alan Slack.

Dr. Slack is a local veterinarian, and his animal hospital sits between his home and the church on Pleasant Street. Dr. Slack and his wife raised seven children, including a set of twins. The Slacks never came to the church, but they were familiar to many in the church and to Earl and Tim, since in addition to ministering at Blessed Hope, they had both lived at one time in the church neighborhood while raising their families. The Slacks were always remembered as good neighbors.

The Slack kids were known as good kids, too. Wade and Andrew worked part-time in the kitchen at the Last Unicorn Restaurant on Silver Street while going to school. Our daughter Erica knew them, as she worked as a waitress there while going to the University of Maine at Farmington. Erica liked and respected these kids. Wade wanted to join the military and planned on entering the army while working at the Unicorn. I remember him wearing a camouflage cap while working in the kitchen before he left for basic training. He reported for basic training in 2007. After basic and then advanced training he became a member of an explosives ordnance disposal (EOD) team.

Deb and I have been regulars at the Unicorn for several years now. Joe Plumstead and his wife, Michelle Cyr, own the restaurant, and they treat all their customers and staff like family. When Dave Grossman came to Waterville to address the law enforcement community of Maine, we had a dinner for him and Joe and Michelle were the persons most responsible for making this dinner happen. It was a Saturday evening and the restaurant does not take reservations on the weekends, but Joe made it happen for the colonel's event anyway.

Deb and I had dinner at the Unicorn on the evening of Thursday, May 6, 2010, where Dr. Slack was also a regular customer. We were not to learn until the next day that one of the Maine Army National Guard chaplains had given notification to Dr. Alan Slack that same evening that his son, United States Army Specialist Wade A. Slack, had been killed in action while serving in Afghanistan earlier that day. Captain Earl Weigelt was soon assigned to minister to the needs of the family.

Earl had participated in those many ramp ceremonies while serving at Kandahar Airfield a few months before, and it was from a similar airfield that Specialist Slack would soon leave Afghanistan for the United States and his waiting family. Captain Weigelt no doubt had a crystal-clear image of the ceremony that would soon occur at the airfield for Specialist Slack, but for now a neighbor's son was dead, a community was stunned, and a family needed ministry—and he would be there to do it.

This was not a family that he had never met before and that he would meet only as a result of the tragedy that had occurred. This was a kid who had grown up next door to where the captain had spent nine years ministering the Gospel, in the neighborhood he had lived in himself. Captain Weigelt's duty would be performed once more, but this time for people that he knew. And he would be there with this family to minister to their needs in whatever way and to whatever extent humanly possible, as well as to seek his God for their comfort.

Dr. Slack soon decided that he wanted his son's funeral to take place at Blessed Hope, and the date selected was Sunday, May 16, 2010, at 2 P.M. Dr. Slack met with Tim Setzer and Captain Weigelt, and plans for the funeral were made. Tim did the introductions, the captain delivered the message, and a community came together for the family of one of their own, a son and an American hero from Waterville, Maine. And it was here that a life was remembered and celebrated, and a sacrifice honored.

There is another church in the United States at this time in our history that actually celebrates the deaths of our soldiers, and even sends their twisted followers to demonstrate at the funerals of the fallen. The protestors from the Westboro Baptist Church often carry signs stating "Thank God for Dead Soldiers." The Independent Baptist Church of Topeka, Kansas, has been credited with sending their followers to military funerals all over the United States, to celebrate the deaths of the soldiers and broadcast their belief that these soldiers have died as a result of God's judgment upon them.

And then there are the Patriot Guard Riders. Their mission statement is as follows, and I quote it from their website:

Patriot Guard Riders Mission Statement

The Patriot Guard Riders is a diverse amalgamation of riders from across the nation. We have one thing in common besides motorcycles. We have an unwavering respect for those who risk their very lives for America's freedom and security. If you share this respect, please join us.

We don't care what you ride or if you ride, what your political views are, or whether you're a hawk or a dove. It is not a requirement that you be a veteran. It doesn't matter where you're from or what your income is; you don't even have to ride. The only prerequisite is Respect.

Our main mission is to attend the funeral services of fallen American heroes *as invited guests of the family*. Each mission we undertake has two basic objectives:

1. Show our sincere respect for our fallen heroes, their families, and their

communities.
2. Shield the mourning family and their friends from interruptions created by any protestor or group of protestors.

We accomplish the latter through strictly legal and non-violent means.

To those of you who are currently serving and fighting for the freedoms of others, at home and abroad, please know that we are backing you. We honor and support you with every mission we carry out, and we are praying for a safe return home for all.

There was some concern that the Westboro protestors would come to Specialist Slack's funeral, so the family extended an invitation to the Patriot Guard Riders to come and take part as invited guests.

The Patriot Guard Riders participated on Friday, May 14, 2010, supplementing the escort law enforcement provided for Wade's body from the airport in Augusta to Veilleux's Funeral Home at 8 Elm Street in Waterville. The Riders stood guard on Saturday, May 15, 2010, during visiting hours at the funeral home. And then on Sunday, May 16, 2010, in addition to the honor guard of the Maine Army National Guard and the presence of local and county law enforcement, the Riders stood guard again at Blessed Hope. And the Westboro Baptist Church protestors did not show.

The winner of six Academy Awards, including Best Picture in 2009, was a film called *The Hurt Locker*, about an EOD team in Iraq. The movie is fiction, but based on the very real and dangerous mission of the EOD teams. Specialist Slack did the stuff that Hollywood can only dream about, in real life, in battle, in Afghanistan, and with honor. If you saw the movie, you know that the EOD teams are targeted by the enemy. The placing of IEDs by the enemy is often a trap for the EOD teams sent to defuse them. The enemy waits for the specialists to arrive and begin their work to make the IED safe, and then they attempt to kill the EOD team. This is what happened to Specialist Slack. He was on such a mission to disarm an IED when his unit was attacked. And remember, it had been an IED that killed Brian Wedge's friend while they were serving in Iraq together in 2003.

According to the article written in the *Waterville Morning Sentinel* covering the details of Wade Slack's funeral, "He died May 6 of wounds suffered from indirect fire in Jaghatu, Afghanistan, after insurgents attacked his Army unit. Slack, who specialized in disarming explosives, was assigned to the 707th Ordnance Company, 3rd Ordnance Battalion, from the Joint Base Lewis-McChord in Washington State."

In attendance, along with Wade's father, Alan, his mother, Mary, his stepmother Rose, and the rest of his grieving family and friends, was United States Senator Olympia Snowe, Governor John Baldacci, Major General John Libby, and other officers and servicemen connected to Wade and his unit. Governor Baldacci presented the Maine Gold Star award and the State House Flag to the family. (The Maine Gold Star is issued in recognition to the families of service men and women killed in combat operations since September 11, 2001.) The United States Army presented Wade with the Combat Action Badge, the NATO Medal, the Purple Heart, and the Bronze Star, all posthumously.

Wade's family and friends remembered Wade from the pulpit. After telling a story about him, his brother Jesse said, "He was my brother, he was my friend; he was my hero." Captain Weigelt read a statement by Wade's sister Lauren. She remarked that Wade "was like glue in our family" and a "true go-getter" who "became Army strong in 2007, but he was strong and determined long before that." The *Morning Sentinel* reported that Major General John Libby "described Slack as the personification of a warrior, which he described as a 'soldier with a heart,' and Slack exemplified the warrior's creed by being a team member who put the mission first and never quit."

This was one of the last funerals at Blessed Hope that Pastor Timothy Setzer took part in before leaving for his new assignment. Tim acted as the host for the event, and Captain Weigelt read the Bible verses selected by Wade's mom, Mary. And the captain told the mourners, in his message, in part, as reported in the *Morning Sentinel*, that "Heroes put their lives on the line. Spc. Wade Alan Slack was such a hero, who died while on a mission to disarm an explosive and save the lives of others, making him also an instrument of peace. So in a very special way, Spc. Wade Slack was a warrior of warriors."

And I know in my heart of hearts that Command Sergeant Major Estol R. McClintock, United States Army, Retired, as well as all the other men from Blessed Hope Church who had also served, would agree that Specialist Wade Alan Slack, United States Army, was a real American hero.

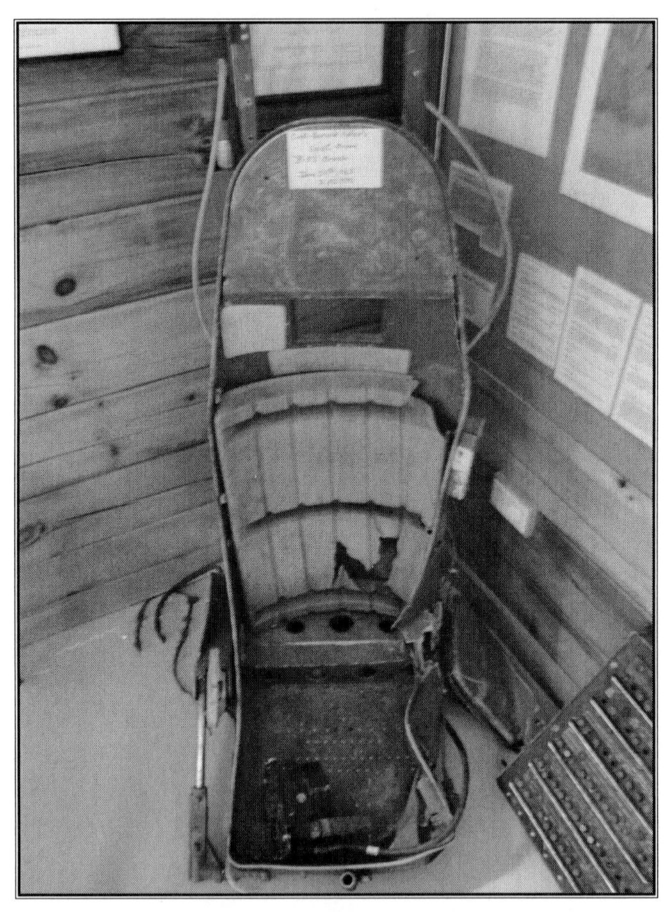

Captain Adler's ejection seat on display at the Moosehead Riders Snowmobile Club. (Photo by Alden Weigelt)

Chapter 16

1400 HRS., MAY 29, 2011, ELEPHANT MOUNTAIN, GREENVILLE, MAINE

A friend of Dr. Alan Slack recently told me that the doctor's biggest fear with regard to his fallen son was that people would eventually forget him.

On October 15, 2010, the Slack family was invited to the Waterville Benevolent and Protective Order of Elks Lodge No. 905 for a memorial service in honor of Wade Slack. About 200 people turned out for the ceremony, including friends, family, city officials, military, law enforcement, and representatives of the Congressional delegation. Debora and I were invited to the ceremony by Dr. Slack, but only I was able to attend that evening.

Captain Earl Weigelt served the family once again, and invoked the presence and comfort of God as well as offering prayer at the ceremony. Kennebec County Sheriff Randall Liberty acted as master of ceremonies. Sheriff Liberty, himself a retired Command Sergeant Major of the United States Army and a veteran of Iraq, wore his army dress uniform for the occasion.

Representing our government were Senators Olympia Snowe and Susan Collins, and U.S. Representative Michael Michaud. They sat with Waterville Mayor Paul LePage, who at the time was a candidate for governor of the State of Maine.

Olympia Snowe remarked that Wade had shown "unfathomable heroism" and that the "U.S. Army, the state, and country had lost a true American hero." In ending her message, she stated, "God bless Wade A. Slack, God bless America, and God bless the entire Slack family."

Susan Collins declared that "It is important that we honor not only the soldier who gave his life for all, but also his family." She added, "It reaffirms our promise to never forget." And then, "To the Slack family, may God, your friends, your neighbors, hold you up in this very difficult time and may God hold you in the palm of his hand."

Congressman Michaud remarked that being at the event was a "humbling experience" for him. He also thanked the Slack family for what they had done to make Wade "what he was."

The Elks presented the Slack family with their Medal of Valor. That evening, a community had occasion to once again remember and honor a life given for others, five months after it was sacrificed.

The day after Debora and I had traveled to visit with Mack and Emaline McClintock that Memorial Day weekend, we traveled to Greenville on Sunday, May 29, 2011, for a memorial service scheduled to take place there that afternoon. Like many Memorial Day weekends I can remember, it was overcast and showers were in the forecast. And somehow the somber weather seemed appropriate for what we were about to appreciate that day. The leader of the event, Peter Pratt, had suggested that Deb and I bring boots, as where we were going was bound to be muddy.

The purpose of this visit was to pay our respects at the ceremony taking place for the sacrifice that had occurred 48 years before on a cold January day on that mountain in Maine. A memorial service for this sacrifice takes place there twice a year. It began in 1993 at the thirtieth anniversary of the crash of Tail Number 53-0406, call sign FROSH 10, on Elephant Mountain in Greenville, Maine. Since that first service 18 years before, and then each following year, there is a memorial service on the date of the crash, January 24th, and a second memorial service on the Sunday before Memorial Day. The amazing thing is that this act of remembrance was not started by a veterans' group or the government. It was started by a snowmobile club.

Fred Worster was the president of the Moosehead Riders Snowmobile Club in 1993, and Fred is credited with having the passion to do something to remember the crew of FROSH 10. Members of the club cleaned up the crash site. They have an informational kiosk set up at their clubhouse on the Scammon Road in Greenville, and the ejection seat that Captain Gerald Adler landed in is on display there. The club organized the events for the thirtieth anniversary of the crash. "On hand for the ceremonies that weekend were state, local and U.S. Air Force officials and two game warden-pilots, who were the first to spot the wreckage and the crewmen on Elephant Mountain," according to a 1993 article by Doug

Harlow in the *Waterville Morning Sentinel.*

Fred Worster passed away some years ago, and Peter "Pete" Pratt is now the B-52 Coordinator for the Moosehead Riders. Pete is passionate about the memory of the sacrifice of the seven lost and the two who survived. It was Peter who had invited Deb and me to the 2011 Memorial weekend service. He told us that every January, during the service, they place seven red roses for each of the men lost in the crash, and explained that they place two yellow roses for the survivors. According to Pete, in recent years, the lady from whom he gets the roses asks him if the count is still seven red and two yellow, as the two survivors are getting up there in age now.

Gerald Adler came for the first memorial service in January of 1993, but Colonel Dante Bulli was unable to attend due to ill health at the time. When Captain Adler returned for that first ceremony on the thirtieth anniversary, he decided to bring the watch that had stopped at 1452 Hrs. on January 24, 1963. Captain Adler told me he had decided to put the watch on and wear it during the flight from California. While on that commercial flight, he said he looked down at the watch and it had started keeping time again.

Pete Pratt told me that he had learned there had been some apprehension about that mission. He said that the usual custom for some members of the crew was to meet their wives at the officers club at the end of a mission. Pete recalled Irene (Morrison) Snyder telling him, when she returned for the memorial service in 2006, that her husband, Major Robert J. Morrison, did not want her to go to the club as usual when he was expected to get back from this particular mission. Instead, the major told his wife he would call her when they arrived home and that they would meet at the club after the call. Captain Adler told me he had put on extra winter clothing that day as had other members of the crew.

I learned from Pete that Irene later married a man by the name of Kenneth Snyder, who was usually the copilot on Robert Morrison's regular flight crew. Kenneth Snyder was not flying the day of the crash. Pete said that when Irene returned with Ken in 2006, it was the first time either of them had visited the crash site. Pete also told me that while visiting the crash site, Ken was very quiet and walked around by himself.

I learned from Captain Adler that Kenneth Snyder was usually the pilot (right seat co-pilot's position as we civilians refer to it) of his regular flight crew, and that Major Morrison was Captain Adler's aircraft commander (left seat pilot's position in civilian aviation) on his regular crew. On the day of the low-level terrain avoidance navigation training exercise, Major Morrison flew in the right seat, and Colonel Bulli was in the left seat as the aircraft commander.

Captain Adler explained that on the day of the mission, those flying were from different crews due to the nature of the training mission. Of those in his regular crew that flew and died that day, were Major Morrison and Captain Charles G. Leuchter, a radar navigator who was flying below deck behind the radar navigator and navigator positions. Leuchter was not in an ejection seat, but as it turned out, that did not matter, as those positions below the flight deck were unable to eject due to the low altitude

Pete told me of a man he knows who, as a young man at the time of the crash, had helped during the recovery efforts in 1963. The man experienced nightmares about the crash and what he had seen for several years. It was not until he returned and experienced one of the memorial services for the first time that he found relief and closure for what had haunted him for so many years.

My father- and mother-in-law, Bill and Betty Lindie, accompanied Debora and me to Greenville on March 30, 2011. There, we met and interviewed Pete for the first time and viewed the information and artifacts of the crash at the Moosehead Riders' clubhouse. I had taken Betty and Bill to the crash site back in 2006. It had been Bill's first visit there since he participated in further recovery efforts of the classified material in the late spring of 1963. During the visit to the site, Bill was very quiet. After that visit to the clubhouse in 2011, Betty told us that Bill had gotten little sleep for the rest of the week. Hearing some of the personal stories of those lost, and of those who had survived had brought all the memories back.

Captain Adler plans to return for another visit to Maine with his family for one of the memorials sometime in the future. Master Sergeant William Lindie looks forward to meeting him, and I am looking forward to meeting him in person.

We accompanied Pete and his wife, Cally, to the crash site for the ceremony on the afternoon of May 29, 2011. The rain held off and there was a glimpse of sun from time to time. On the drive up, Pete explained that he had been to the site a few days earlier to look things over and collect the roses from the ceremony in January. Interestingly, he had found in excess of $34.00 in loose change that someone had left before snowfall in 2010 at the base of the Monson slate memorial. He added the money to the B-52 memorial fund at the clubhouse. When Pete and Cally go to the crash site, they often find several visitors, and the usual demeanor of the visitors is one of quiet respect.

We arrived at the site and were joined by some others. The Greenville chapter of the American Legion was on hand with a firing party for a gun salute, and their chaplain offered a prayer. After the prayer and gun salute, taps were played on a portable CD player. Those in attendance had the opportunity to quietly reflect on the debris field that marks and still scars the landscape. Pete refers to the area as being sacred, "like a grave"... and it is.

There are still those who remember, and my faith has been restored by this example of everyday citizens who do not allow this sacred memory of sacrifice to die or this sacred place to be forgotten or desecrated. May those who follow preserve them both.

I hope that Dr. Slack and others like him can be reassured that there will always be those who remember their sons who gave all that man can give.

Chapter 17

REMEMBERING THE GIFT

I hope the events and people I have chronicled have caused you to reflect on some of the everyday lives you may know or have heard of in your own circle of family and acquaintances. These people and the reminders that point to them are all around us, if only we open our eyes. We owe them so much. Of course, these examples of sacrifice are not specific only to Maine, and if you live somewhere else in our great land, you can find them there, too. And, of course, this is not the complete story, nor could it be. I have left some doors open purposely in the hope that you will hunger to learn more about some of those around you.

The 1998 movie directed by Steven Spielberg, *Saving Private Ryan*, is a fictional story about a squad of soldiers sent to find a paratrooper a few days after D-Day. The young paratrooper in the story is the sole surviving son of his family back home. His three brothers have been killed fighting in World War II, and Army Chief of Staff George C. Marshall has just learned of this and decides that Private James Francis Ryan must be saved for the sake of his mother and the rest of his family. Though the movie is fiction, it is, just the same, one of the most graphic portrayals of combat on Omaha Beach ever re-created for the screen.

If you never saw the movie, but the plot somehow sounds familiar, you may recall Estol (Mack) McClintock from earlier pages of this book. You'll remember that Mack had refused the Congressional Order to send him home after his only brother was killed during the Battle of the Bulge. Like so many other veterans, Mack never watched *Saving Private Ryan*—and for so many other reasons.

At the end of the movie, the squad sent to save Private Ryan is almost completely wiped out, with the exception of one of the squad members and Captain Miller (played by Tom Hanks), who was sent to lead his men in the search for Ryan. Miller has been mortally wounded, and in this scene is sitting on the ground dying, while the other squad member calls for a medic. Private Ryan, played by Matt Damon, leans down in despair over the wounds to the captain, and Captain Miller speaks to him in a whisper that only Ryan can hear: "James, earn this...earn it," and then he dies.

The scene then returns the audience to the present day and the place where the movie began, the Normandy American Cemetery overlooking Omaha Beach. Private Ryan is again an old man, and we learn that he has brought his wife, son, daughter-in-law, and grandchildren here to visit for the first time. He finds the grave of the captain who, with the other men, gave their lives to save him.

Ryan's wife has evidently heard the story of Captain Miller, as she says to her husband after reading his name on the stone cross, "He's the one." While standing in front of Captain Miller's grave, James Ryan asks his wife to tell him that he has led a good life and that he has been a good man. An old man is humbled and haunted by the sacrifice made for him by others, and appreciates the gift given to him for a long life. We learn that the old man has thought of little else than "earning" the gift given him, every day of his life since.

And now it is time for *us* to remember the sacrifice. On Tuesday, June 28, 2011, an article in the *Waterville Morning Sentinel* titled "Maine's Rate of War Dead Ranks High" confirmed once again that the motto of the Great State of Maine, *Dirigo*, is true. The article, supported by an article in *The Guardian* newspaper of England and based on casualty figures released by the U.S. Department of Defense for the 10th year of Operation Enduring Freedom in Afghanistan, states that the ratio of Maine soldiers killed to the population of the State of Maine is higher than any other state in our nation. And during the Civil War, as you may recall, Maine had the most volunteers in ratio to draftees that served than any other state in the Union.

If you want to see an illustration of the ratio of sheep (citizens) to sheepdogs (warriors), walk through a rural Maine cemetery the weekend of Memorial Day. As you look over the silent reminders, note the flags above those who chose to serve and stand in the way for those who could not or would not stand there for themselves. You may even write down a name and choose to learn more. There is a cemetery in Lincoln, Maine, that I would point you to next Memorial Day weekend. There you will find many names to learn about. There is one name there that you may consider starting with. He is Gary Gordon and it wasn't so very long ago.

And please remember once more that Maine is only one of fifty states in our great nation that have sent warriors in harm's way for "the sacred cause of justice and the freedom of the world." Statistics are somewhat hard to narrow down sometimes, and what follows is my best attempt, from the data I was able to locate, at an illustration of the sacrifice of our American Warriors from all across the nation during some of the major conflicts dating from today back to the Civil War.

Afghanistan and Iraq	6,118 American Warriors killed
Persian Gulf War	294 American Warriors killed
Vietnam	58,655 American Warriors killed
Korea	54,246 American Warriors killed
WW II	407,316 American Warriors killed
WW I	116,708 American Warriors killed
Civil War	618,000 American Warriors killed

The following represents the ratio of American Warriors killed to the total population of the United States at the time of their sacrifice for us.

Afghanistan and Iraq	1 Warrior for every 50,465 American citizens
Gulf War	1 Warrior for every 845,951 American citizens
Vietnam	1 Warrior for every 3,466 American citizens
Korea	1 Warrior for every 2,789 American citizens
WW II	1 Warrior for every 324 American citizens
WW I	1 Warrior for every 908 American citizens
Civil War	1 Warrior for every 50 American citizens

Now is the time for every American citizen to realize how much has been sacrificed for them, a time for every American to live a life worthy of the sacrifice of those who have given all that he or she had to give. It is time to validate that sacrifice. It is time for each one of us to consider what it means to earn this thing we call "Freedom," and to live the rest of our lives in honor of it.

To the American Warrior, I pray we remain forever thankful and forever grateful for your service. May God bless and keep you and yours, and for those who have already passed now, may they be remembered always until He returns for us all.

Amen.

Westminster Abbey Garden of Remembrance. (Photo by Alden Weigelt)

Epilogue

REMEMBRANCE SUNDAY, NOVEMBER 14, 2010, WHITEHALL

In 2010, Deb and I were invited by our friend Ken McGrath to London for the ceremonies observing the 11th of November. We have been traveling to England now for several years and, in addition to Ken, we have two friends from the British Transport Police who had served as counterterror specialists. The year after we met them, the London bombings occurred on July 7, 2005, perpetrated by the same evil ideology as that which inspired the September 11th attacks in the United States. Brian and Russell are veterans of that infamous day, and both of them know and understand what it means to be a "sheepdog." (I am not including their correct or full names for obvious reasons.)

The 11th of November is a day of particular significance to France, Belgium, the United States, and the United Kingdom. It marks the end of World War I, or the Great War as it was known at the time. At the 11th hour of the 11th day of the 11th month in 1918, the Allies signed the armistice agreement with Germany. Two short decades later, Great Britain and the United States would come to France and Belgium once more for the freedom of the world.

Armistice Day, as it was originally called, was a day to remember the dead of World War I. It was later changed to Veterans Day in the United States, and is now a day to honor all veterans. In Great Britain and the Commonwealth, it was changed to Remembrance Day, and is now a day to remember all members of their armed forces who have died on duty since World War I.

The Green Howard's Section of the Garden. Remembering Wade and Elmer. (Photo by Alden Weigelt)

Ken McGrath is one of Her Majesty's Yeoman Warders of Her Majesty's Royal Palace and Fortress, the Tower of London. The Yeoman Warders are the guardians of the Tower and the Crown Jewels. Yes, they provide tours to the tourists, but make no mistake: that is not their main purpose. They stand watch 24 hours a day and are supplemented by armed elements of the British Army. When the tourists leave and the gates are locked, the Tower is most secure and is in very capable hands.

To be a Yeoman Warder, one must have served honorably as a senior noncommissioned officer in the British Army, the Royal Air Force, or the Royal Marines for at least 22 years. The application process is exhaustive, and those selected have impeccable character and service records. There are only thirty-five Yeoman Warders, and their history and tradition date back about 700 years. The Yeoman Warders, or "Beefeaters," as they are sometimes called, live at the Tower with their families.

Ken had served in the British Army with his regiment, the Green Howards, and he is a combat veteran. Ken retired as a Company Sergeant Major (Warrant Officer Class 2) of the Green Howards. And, like Estol McClintock, he is not all that tall. Also like Estol McClintock, you never picture him in your mind as short. And like Mack, he is tough as nails. In addition to his duties at the Tower, Ken also serves as a reserve police officer with the London Metropolitan Police.

The regiments of the British Army are steeped in tradition. And their members are very proud of their history and traditions, as well they should be. Ken's regiment, the Green Howards, was first raised as a regiment in 1688, and they are still serving today since being amalgamated with two other regiments in 2006 to form the new Yorkshire Regiment. The Coldstream Guards are the oldest continually serving regiment in the British Army. They have been serving faithfully since 1650. If you do the math, you realize that we went up against them both and their other regiments in 1776 and 1812. Then we stood beside them in 1917 and 1941. Then *they* stood beside *us* in 1991 and 2001, and they continue to stand with us today.

Ken likes to rub it in from time to time that there is a rumor that it might have been his regiment, the Green Howards, that was responsible for burning down the White House during the War of 1812 and running James and Dolly Madison out of town. In response, I'm fond of reminding him that he is a descendant of arsonists. This conversation usually results in a good-natured argument over the insistence by one of us to buy the other the next round of lager or ale.

The purpose of this trip in 2010 was to pay our respects, and in doing so, remember...with our British friends. At Westminster Abbey, that great thousand-year-old house of worship, there is a memorial "garden" formed each November on the grounds. Each military regiment or unit of the armed forces is assigned a section of the lawn on which to place wooden crosses bearing the names of their dead. The crosses are about six inches tall and have a paper poppy in the center. The person placing the cross writes on it the name of the person to be remembered. The garden remains each year into the month of December.

On the evening of the 12th, we met up with Ken and about fifteen members of the Green Howards Association at the memorial garden for a service and prayers. It was appropriate that it was raining. After the service, we went to New Scotland Yard for a reception and supper, and then on to a local pub. Ken then asked me if I would march with the Green Howards on Remembrance Sunday, when all the veterans march down Whitehall after the Queen and other members of the Royal Family have laid their wreaths at the monument known as the Cenotaph. (Ken shares my love of history, and our conversations often turn to it. It was during our time together this week that Ken suggested I write this book.)

Later in the week, Ken gave Deb and me two crosses to place in the Green Howards' section of the garden for those we wanted to remember. We wrote the names of two men from Maine and placed them with the crosses of the Howards' dead. These men had served at the same time as our British allies and one of them was killed in action while serving. In 2010, they were both remembered with the British at their place of honor. On one cross, we wrote: "Wade Slack, U.S. Army" and indicated his service in Afghanistan in 2010. On the other cross, we wrote: "Elmer Lindie, U.S. Army," and indicated that he had served in WW I.

On the morning of November 14, 2010, Remembrance Sunday, Deb waited for the ceremony to begin in front of the Foreign Office and the Cenotaph, where Ken had suggested she stand. Deb was to stand behind the present and former prime ministers, and was about 20 feet away from them. The Queen's Scouts formed the line that the Queen walked out through, and Debora was right behind them and was as close as 20 feet from Her Majesty, Queen Elizabeth II, and the other members of the Royal Family when they came out for the ceremony. Exiting the Foreign Office with the Queen was her husband, Prince Phillip, Duke of Edinburgh, as well as Charles, Prince of Wales; Prince Andrew, Duke of York; Prince Edward, Earl of Wessex; Anne, the Princess Royal; and Prince Edward, Duke of Kent and first cousin to Queen Elizabeth. Prince William was not there, as he was in Afghanistan observing Remembrance Sunday with the troops.

I had formed up on Horse Guards Parade with about fifteen of the Green Howards. We were in column A of the formation organized by the Royal British Legion. The Royal British Legion is the British veterans' organization and is similar to our American Legion. There were three Green Howard Brigadiers (brigadier generals) with us who had arrived with a few other officers. The officers did not know who I was, and when Ken introduced me as an American police officer, there were comments such as "good show" as I met them. I was very warmly welcomed. We also had occasion for some conversation before the formation moved out.

We marched out onto Whitehall through the archway of Horse Guards Parade six abreast, and I was on the extreme right of the column. There were several thousand civilians waiting for us when we emerged and halted on Whitehall in preparation for the ceremony to begin—and the crowd broke out into cheers and applause for their veterans.

The day was overcast, and at times, it sprinkled. A flyover of the Royal Air Force had been planned, but it was not to happen due to the weather. But the weather was somehow appropriate for what this ceremony was all about.

The Cenotaph Eyes...Left! (Photo by Debora Weigelt)

While standing in formation, there was the gentle and good-natured bantering that always occurs between warriors. I heard some catcalls in regard to "the Budgies are here, the Budgies are here." Former Green Howard bugler, Robert Purvis, asked me if I knew who the regiment in front of us was, and I responded that I didn't. Robert told me that the chaps ahead of us in the formation were the Royal Regiment of Fusiliers, and pointed out that they were the only unit to wear a plume with their hat device and beret. He said that they refer to the Fusiliers as the "Budgie Brigade" because of their feather plumes. Then the soldier became deadly serious and showed his deepest respect for them while explaining that the "Budgies" have a red tip on their plumes because of an incident during one of several famous battles in their long and honored history. In that battle with the French, they took the plumes from the French dead, dipped them in their blood, and then placed them on their own hats.

We stood in formation on Whitehall for the laying of the wreaths, the Lord's Prayer, and several hymns. There was also a two-minute moment of silence beginning at the stroke of 1100 Hrs. by the famous bell, Big Ben, in the clock tower of the Palace of Westminster. I thought of Specialist Slack, and of the young Royal Navy pilots buried and the two still missing in Maine. And this was a Christian service. Remember, Her Majesty has "Defender of the Faith" as part of her title. The Sovereign is also head of the Church of England, and there was no doubt that the presence of our Lord was felt there by many.

The final song was "God Save the Queen," and all sang the British national anthem. While this tribute to Her Majesty was sung, I could not help thinking of the significance of the connection between the First Baptist Church in my own hometown and the song "My Country, 'Tis of Thee." I felt a deep sense of camaraderie in the realization that our great nations share this piece of music, which is both similar and different, and yet at the same time sacred to both our countries.

After the wreaths were laid, we stepped off and began marching to the tune of "It's a Long Way to Tipperary." We marched down Whitehall toward the Cenotaph and then marched to the right side of the monument. Ken had reminded me to "march like an Englishman," and we all marched, enlisted and officers, including even generals, to Ken's parade commands and cadence. As we reached the Cenotaph, Ken ordered: "Green Howards...eyes...left!" and we snapped our heads to the left in salute to that great monument that bears witness without shame to Britain's "Glorious Dead."

Deb was able to capture this moment on camera as we passed by the place where, only moments before, Her Majesty The Queen had paid her most solemn respects. It should be noted that this is one of the few times the Sovereign bows her head, and it is to the dead who have given all that man can give, life itself.

A short distance away, in Westminster Abbey, the Unknown Warrior of Britain was laid to rest around the same time that the Cenotaph was erected, after the Great War and just before our own Unknown Soldier from the same war was laid to rest in Arlington. On his tombstone, where he is buried in this house of worship with many of the kings and queens of England, are inscribed these words:

...THE MOST THAT MAN CAN GIVE LIFE ITSELF FOR GOD FOR KING AND COUNTRY FOR LOVED ONES HOME AND EMPIRE FOR THE SACRED CAUSE OF JUSTICE AND THE FREEDOM OF THE WORLD...

We continued past the Cenotaph and the thousands on the street behind the barricades. They never ceased applauding as we marched by. Again, I was on the extreme right of the six-across formation and right next to the people as we passed. There was pride, respect, and emotion

The Green Howards and an American police officer. (Photo courtesy of Ken McGrath)

everywhere in their expressions as we passed.

We reached Parliament Square, turned right, and proceeded onto Great George Street. We continued on until we reached Horse Guards Road and turned right onto it. All the while, the people applauded and cheered. As we approached Horse Guards Parade, we saw Princess Anne, who had been positioned to receive our salute. Years before, Princess Anne had resisted a kidnapping attempt by a deranged man who had attacked her vehicle with a firearm, shooting her bodyguard, her driver, and a bystander who had come to assist her. When the man ordered the Princess to get out of the car, she responded, "Not bloody likely!"

The Princess stood on a small dais right next to where I would soon march by. Her right hand was in the position of salute, palm out. She held that salute as more than 7000 marched past. When Ken gave the next command, I was within ten feet of the Princess. Ken commanded: "Green Howards...eyes...right!" As my head snapped right, I did as we'd been instructed to do and looked Her Highness in the eye. As our eyes met there was immediate acknowledgment and respect in hers, and by this time there was probably some mist in mine.

We continued and marched onto the Parade to form up again before being dismissed. After Ken halted the Howards, he ordered: "Green Howards...right...turn!" Perfectly, as one unit, we did as instructed. Then Ken ordered us to "Stand...at...ease!" and we applauded the other veterans as they arrived and formed in row upon row beside us.

There were those who had recently seen action. Some were in wheelchairs and many had no legs. One young trooper had no legs and no eyes, but had a grin while speaking with his mates. There were the old guys, too, and you knew where and when they had served by just looking at them. Then there were the Ghurkas, and let's not forget the Red Devils, either. One old Red Devil was having trouble keeping up, but finished the march with his fellow paratroopers. Warriors all!

This was one of the proudest and most humbling days of my life, but it was far from over. After the parade, Ken had arranged for the Howards to have lunch at a local pub. We met up with Deb and the other ladies from our group. After lunch, we all went to the Royal Hospital, the home of the Chelsea Pensioners, to fellowship with the pensioners in their club. There were many friends and family members of the pensioners there as well. We drank and talked all afternoon, and as evening approached, some of the tables broke out in song. This lack of inhibition was only and entirely due to the warm fellowship experienced by all. Right...that's it. Our table sang as well, and there seemed to be some friendly competition between the tables.

One of the old gentlemen, who seemed to be the leader at the next table, was dressed in green slacks and a sweater that matched. He was very happy, as well as emotional, and was leading the singing, at times singing solo. During a break, he came over to me and asked who I was. I explained that I was not military but only an American police officer, and that I was there as a guest of the Howards. The gentleman acknowledged this and seemed to be glad I was there.

A few minutes later, he returned with tears in his eyes as well as some on his cheeks. He asked me if I would be offended if he gave me something. I looked down and he had neatly folded his green nylon jacket with the crest of the Durham Light Infantry on it. He put it in my hands. I stopped the gentleman, explaining to him again that I was not military and asking if he understood this. The gentleman explained that it was *because* I was an American police officer that he was doing this, and that I only needed to promise that I would never forget the Durham Light Infantry. I then learned that their regiment has been amalgamated with so many others of the British Army that they no longer exist as an individual regiment anymore. I also knew the importance the history and traditions of the regiments hold for their members.

The old gentleman was the chairman of the Durham Light Infantry Association. I told the old gentleman that I would only accept the jacket if it were with the understanding that we agreed together that we did the same thing. I told him that he was the tip of the spear and I was the shield and that together we both stood in the way for others who could not or would not stand there for themselves. I told him of the wolves and the sheep and asked him to remember we were sheepdogs. The old warrior understood this concept very well. We parted, both with just moist eyes now and the knowledge that we share the eternal bond...of brother warriors.

Bibliography

Adler, Jerry. "The Elephant Mountain Incident." In *We Were Crewdogs V: We Flew the Heavies*, edited by Tommy Towery. Memphis: Tommy Towery, 2009, 107–114.

——. "Survivor Says 'Heavenly Co-Pilot' Guided Him." *Bangor Daily News*, September 23, 1967.

Associated Press. "Colby Joins Strike." *Waterville Morning Sentinel*, May 7, 1970.

——. "Protests Multiply on U.S. Campuses." *Waterville Morning Sentinel*, May 9, 1970.

——. "Sit-In Ends at Colby's ROTC Area." *Waterville Morning Sentinel*, May 9, 1970.

Calder, Amy. "Soldier's sacrifice honored: Wade Slack's family receives Medal of Valor at Waterville ceremony." *Waterville Morning Sentinel*, October 16, 2010. http://www.onlinesentinel.com.

Chamberlain, Joshua Lawrence. *Bayonet! Forward: My Civil War Reminiscences.* Gettysburg: Stan Clark Military Books, 1994.

"The Churchill Centre and Museum at the Churchill War Rooms, London" at http://www.winstonchurchill.org.

Colby Echo. "Colby on Strike!!" May 8, 1970. http://digital.olivesoftware.com.

The Dean and Chapter of St. Paul's Cathedral. "St. Paul's Cathedral" at http://www.stpauls.co.uk.

Ferland, Durward. "On a Mountain in Maine: The crash of a B-52 StratoFortress." *Up North, the Moosehead Magazine,* January/February 2006, 40–43.

"Fleet Air Arm Archive, 1939–1945" at http://fleetairarmarchive.net/Squadrons/USA.htm.

Graves, David. "Palace breaks with tradition in musical tribute." *The Telegraph*, September 14, 2001. http://www.telegraph.co.uk.

Harlow, Doug. "Ceremonies mark crash anniversary." *Waterville Morning Sentinel*, January 25, 1993.

Harriman, Pamela, from an interview by Martin Gilbert. "Churchill: To Conquer or to Die." *A&E Biography.* A&E Television Networks, 1991.

Homes, Marian, from an interview by Martin Gilbert. "Churchill: To Conquer or to Die." *A&E Biography.* A&E Television Networks, 1991.

Jordan, Glenn. "Maine's rate of war dead ranks high." *Waterville Morning Sentinel*, June 28, 2011.

Keeney, L. Douglas. *15 Minutes: General Curtis LeMay and the Countdown to Nuclear Annihilation.* New York: St. Martin's Press, 2011.

Kelso, Paul. "US anthem played at changing of the guard." *The Guardian*, September 14, 2001. http://www.guardian.co.uk.

King, Angus. "Remarks by Maine State Governor Angus King delivered at Bowdoin's Commencement." *Bowdoin Campus News*, May 25, 1996. http://www.bowdoin.edu.

Korda, Michael. *With Wings Like Eagles: The Untold Story of the Battle of Britain.* New York: Harper Perennial, 2009.

"Maine Civil War Monuments: Waterville (Colby Library)" at State of Maine website: http://www.maine.gov/civilwar/monuments/waterville-colby.html.

"Maine Civil War Monuments: Waterville (Old Colby College)" at State

of Maine website.
http://www.maine.gov/civilwar/monuments/watervilleoldcolby.html.

McKinstry, Norman. "A British Cadet's Odyssey to NAS Grosse Ile and Beyond." HMS *Vengeance* at http://www.hms-vengeance.co.uk/nmckinst.htm.

Monroe, Scott. "'He was an incredible soldier.' Relatives, friends, fellow soldier recall Wade Slack as always cheerful." *Waterville Morning Sentinel*, May 17, 2010. http://www.onlinesentinel.com.

Noddin, Pete. "Aviation Archaeology in Maine" at http://mewreckchasers.com.

Northway, Mike. "The Civil War Archive" at http://www.civilwararchive.com.

Saunders, Andy. "Corsairs in the Lake." *Britain at War Magazine*, December 2009, 19–26.

Shettleworth, Earle G., Jr. "Maine Compass: Maine's Significant Contribution to Civil War." *Waterville Morning Sentinel*, April 10, 2011.

Smith, Sally Bedell. *Elizabeth The Queen: The Life of a Modern Monarch.* New York:
Random House, 2012.

Smith, Star. *Jimmy Stewart, Bomber Pilot.* Minneapolis: Zenith Press, 2006.

Swank, Ryan, and Tennessee Watson. "Colby activism during the Vietnam War." *Colby Echo*, February 20, 2003. http://digital.olivesoftware.com.

Time Magazine. "Prisoners of War: Bittersweet Homecoming of Three Pilots." October 9, 1972. http://www.time.com.

United States Navy. "USS *Winston S. Churchill*" at http://www.churchill.navy.mil.

Waterville Morning Sentinel. "Fails to Ignite: Fire Bomb Tossed Into

Colby Office." May 25, 1970.

——. "Over 400 at Colby: Students Demonstrate on Campus, Downtown." May 6, 1970.

——. "The Maine Scene: Curtis Proclaims Day of Mourning." May 8, 1970.

Index

About the Author

Alden L. Weigelt is a veteran police officer from Central Maine. He currently serves as a patrol officer for the City of Waterville. Weigelt has specialized training from the FBI as a crisis negotiator. He is also a certified police firearms instructor as well as a licensed emergency medical technician. Alden still enjoys general aviation as a private pilot. He lives in Central Maine with his wife Debora, where they are both active in their church. They have three children and five grandchildren with number six on the way.